HOW WE PRACTICE

AN INTRODUCTION TO MEDITATION

SACRAMENTO INSIGHT MEDITATION

Jeff Hardin

Sacramento, California

DHAMMACAKKA PRESS

SACRAMENTO INSIGHT MEDITATION

Sacramento Insight Meditation (SIM) is a non-profit organization that supports insight meditation training and practice in the Sacramento area. Our group bases its practices on the teachings of the historical Buddha as passed down through generations of meditation teachers and practitioners in the Theravadan Buddhist lineage. A range of teachings are offered at SIM including insight meditation (also known as *vipassana* or mindfulness meditation), lovingkindness (*metta*) meditation, body scan meditation, yoga, formal study of Buddhist texts, spiritual friends *(kalyana mitta)* support groups, and volunteer work. With the guidance of senior dharma teacher John Travis our founding instructor, Dennis Warren, formed SIM in 2002. SIM provides support for meditation practitioners regardless of age, gender, sexual orientation, religious affiliation, race, or economic status. We are an all-volunteer group that is cooperatively guided by a board of directors and an instructional team consisting of community-trained mentors. No membership dues or fees are required and all programs are funded by voluntary donations (*dana*) from community members. Donations are used for operational expenses (rent, supplies, etc.) and to support special programs such as daylong retreats, classes, and visits by senior insight meditation teachers. SIM meets regularly for group meditation and a dharma talk, monthly daylong meditation retreats, and an annual residential retreat.

"All conditioned things are subject to decay. Practice diligently."

–The Buddha

TABLE OF CONTENTS

INTRODUCTION

"Doing no harm,
Engaging in what's skillful,
And purifying one's mind:
This is the teaching of the Buddhas."

-Dhp 183

Insight meditation, also known as *vipassana* meditation, is a form of mindfulness meditation that calms the mind, allowing its innate wisdom to produce insights into the nature of our existence. It is based on the teachings of the historical Buddha who lived 2500 years ago. The teachings have been handed down by generations of meditation practitioners, initially in India where the Buddha lived, but eventually throughout the world. This book is intended as a primer to the practice of meditation as it is taught at the Sacramento Insight Meditation (SIM) group in Sacramento, California. As an introduction to meditation it is meant to support and encourage you, the reader, to take up the practice of meditation and to see if meditation is a worthwhile activity in your life. It is not meant as a definitive guide to meditation or as a substitute for experiential practice. You are encouraged to work within a meditation group such as SIM and to receive personal guidance from a skillful meditation teacher(s). The views and opinions expressed in the book are my own and I am responsible for any errors or omissions. There are many meditation styles and techniques available; this book covers a few of these methods. I have found these techniques most useful in my own exploration of meditation and in my efforts to live a balanced, harmonious, and happy life. I hope you find them useful as well.

"With firm resolve, guard your own mind!"

- DN 16

At SIM we practice and teach more than just how to meditate. When the Buddha's teachings (the **Dhamma** in *Pali*, *Dharma* in *Sanskrit*) are studied and applied to one's life we find that every aspect of how we live in this world can be affected for the better. When the practice of meditative awareness is developed and brought to bear on our lives, we see many positive benefits: 1) we are more connected with our experience and more present in our lives; 2) relationships are enhanced – there is greater intimacy with other people, animals, and the environment; 3) our deepest intentions as human beings are investigated and purposefully developed; 4) areas in our life that are difficult or painful, or where we are harming ourselves or others are explored and, when it is beneficial, changes are implemented; Skillful behaviors are developed while unskillful ones are abandoned; and 5) we learn to accept our own illnesses and mortality and face death with courage and peace.

Meditative awareness is a skill that can be intentionally developed and applied usefully to every aspect of our lives. At the heart of meditative awareness is **mindfulness**. There are many historical and conventional definitions of mindfulness but at SIM we define it as non-judgmental, present-moment awareness. This is a quality of attention that is based in the present moment that is free from the interpretations, commentaries, judgments, memories, planning, and the likes and dislikes that we usually bring to our experience. We are directly connected with our bare experience and attentive to the constant change occurring in each moment. Developing the skill of mindfulness allows us to learn to become free from our usual habitual reactivity to experience and to be present for whatever is happening with a calm, balanced mind. Out of mindfulness our innate wisdom and compassion blossoms. This allows us to live in the world with harmony, integrity, skill, and peace. We cease harming ourselves and others and no longer contribute to the mass of suffering in the world. Full development of the skill of mindfulness supports the cultivation of a wisdom that ends our suffering and stress permanently. This liberation or awakening (*Nibbana* in *Pali*, *Nirvana* in *Sanskrit*) is the goal of the Buddha's teachings.

The word for mindfulness in *Pali* is "*sati*," which is also the word for memory. This emphasizes that we must constantly remember to be with our experience in the present moment and without judgment or interpretation. Like any skill (such as playing a sport or musical instrument), developing mindfulness requires practice. In order to break our old, unskillful habitual mental patterns and develop new, skillful mindfulness-based ones we must repeatedly return our awareness to the present moment without judging it. The practice is really nothing more than returning our attention again and again to our experience of the moment, with acceptance. As you read through this book the various practices may seem overwhelming. If pursued all at once from the beginning of one's practice, they would be. However, a gradual path was taught by the Buddha and at SIM we recommend starting with the basic instructions for sitting meditation. After practicing for a while, this foundation is built upon by refining the existing techniques and introducing new ones. As with all skills, the results obtained are proportional to the amount of effort invested. In order to optimize one's success in beginning a meditation practice it is best to commit to a period of practice of several weeks to several months. During this time period it is ideal to practice the techniques with patience and consistency. It is best to practice meditation daily. As mindfulness skills are developed over time, many find that practice becomes easier and meditation becomes an integral part of life.

WHY MEDITATE?

"Through effort, vigilance,
Restraint, and self-control,
The wise person can become an island
No flood will overwhelm."

- Dhp. 25

Before embarking on a meditation practice it is useful to reflect on your reasons for wanting to meditate. Embracing meditative awareness in your life and committing to regular practice of meditation requires a significant commitment of time and energy. Although most people find immediate and long-term benefits to meditation, there can be periods of difficulty, painful insights, boredom, frustration, anxiety, grief, and significant internal and external changes in your life resulting from meditation practice. For these reasons, it is important to have a clear idea for yourself why you want to meditate. If you have not done so already, please reflect for a while on why you have decided to pursue meditation. It can be helpful to write out a list of reasons that you can refer to later in your practice.

The following is a list of some of the reasons why people meditate: 1) meditation can improve physical and mental health; 2) it improves concentration and memory; 3) it allows us to be more helpful and kinder to ourselves and others; 4) it reduces stress, fear, and anxiety; 5) it reduces chronic pain and helps people cope better with chronic ailments; 6) it improves connectivity to family and friends; 7) it provides a belief system and a blueprint for living that many people find comforting and skillful; 8) it shifts the focus from a chaotic and unmanageable external world toward a peaceful and stable internal one; 9) it promotes self-awareness and self-acceptance; 10) it reduces insomnia, helping people to sleep more deeply, and to require less sleep; and 11) it increases one's appreciation for life. Having listed some benefits of meditation, it is important to know that not everyone experiences all of these. However, most people who invest the time in developing the skill of meditation find it a highly worthy endeavor.

THE 3 TRAININGS

"If, by giving up a lesser happiness,
One could experience greater happiness,
A wise person would renounce the lesser
To behold the greater."

- Dhp. 290

The Buddha did not teach meditation in isolation. He taught the development of meditation as one aspect of developing the mind and body. In many of the discourses (*Pali suttas*) he stated the goal of his teaching to be the understanding of and elimination of stress and suffering in our lives. That meant, and he stated explicitly, that he did not teach a metaphysical belief system, palliative rituals, magic tricks, theology, or a world philosophy. His teachings were pragmatic and aimed directly toward the goal of eliminating stress and suffering. To achieve this goal the Buddha taught 3 trainings that are to be practiced simultaneously: ethical conduct (*sila*), concentration/meditation (*samadhi*), and wisdom (*panna*). These 3 trainings are further divided into 8 specific areas of practice: **The Noble Eightfold Path** describes the complete Buddhist path of practice. He called it the Middle Way between indulgence in sensual desire and self-neglect. Each of the factors of the noble eightfold path is called skillful. This word comes from the *Pali* term "*samma*." *Samma* can be translated as skillful, wholesome, wise, healthy, or right. While practicing the 3 trainings it is important always to balance our effort so that it is neither too slack nor too stern.

Over the centuries since the time of the Buddha, many people have tried to develop meditation without the aid of the other two trainings (*sila* and *panna*). This greatly reduces the efficacy of meditation. At SIM, meditation is taught as one important component of the 3 trainings. The 8 factors of the 3 trainings are listed in Table 1.

Table 1: The Three Trainings and the Noble Eightfold Path

Training	Noble Eightfold Path Factor
Ethical Conduct (*sila*)	Skillful Speech (*samma vaca*)
	Skillful Action (*samma kammanta*)
	Skillful Livelihood (*samma ajiva*)
Concentration (*samadhi*)	Skillful Effort (*samma vayama*)
	Skillful Mindfulness (*samma sati*)
	Skillful Concentration (*samma samadhi*)
Wisdom (*panna*)	Skillful View (*samma ditthi*)
	Skillful Intention (*samma sankappa*)

1. TRAINING IN ETHICAL CONDUCT (SKILLFUL SPEECH, ACTION, AND LIVELIHOOD)

"If you hold yourself dear
then don't fetter yourself with harmful actions,
for happiness isn't easily gained
by one who commits harm."

- SN

Some people question the importance of ethical conduct in developing a meditation practice. However, it takes little experience to see how directly our actions affect the quality of our mind and body. For example, injuring others disturbs the mind and creates tension in the body. We may experience remorse over our actions and/or fear retribution. This is counterproductive to the calm, concentration, and balance required for meditation. Although most religions base their ethics on the concept of good versus evil, Buddhism bases its ethics on the concept of cause and effect. That is, when we perform unskillful, harmful acts, suffering results. When we do skillful, beneficial acts, happiness and peace result. The foundation of all Buddhist practice is the cultivation of **non-harming** of ourselves and others. Although this seems like a straightforward and even simple principle, it has far-reaching and deep implications for our practice and our lives. To live an ethically sound life, the Buddha recommended **5 training precepts**. These are not meant as commandments or absolutes, rather they are offered as guides to help us act skillfully in the world, as areas of self-inquiry, and as a framework to measure our progress on the spiritual path. The 5 precepts are worded to remind us that they are training precepts and not laws:

1. **I undertake the training precept to refrain from killing.**
2. **I undertake the training precept to refrain from taking what is not given.**
3. **I undertake the training precept to refrain from sexual misconduct.**
4. **I undertake the training precept to refrain from lying.**
5. **I undertake the training precept to refrain from intoxicating drinks and drugs that lead to heedlessness.**

With each of these we are asked not to follow them blindly, but to investigate them and to make them an area of active meditative exploration in our lives. The Buddha recommended that we constantly ask ourselves, "Which of my actions, speech, or thoughts lead to welfare and happiness and which lead to suffering and harm?" This should be done before, during, and after embarking on anything. It is important that our actions be considered for their consequences on ourselves and on others. Understanding the interdependency and conditional nature of all things is essential to awakening (see "dependent origination," page 79). When ethical conduct is developed as a skill, a very rich area of inquiry that produces ongoing positive effects is opened in our lives. Each precept deserves investigation and development. When we practice with all 5 simultaneously we have a means for living a wholesome, balanced, and beneficial life. What follows are brief descriptions of each precept and points of inquiry for practice.

1. **I undertake the training precept to refrain from killing.** To refrain from killing is perhaps the most important action we can take. It may be obvious that killing other humans is harmful to them and can lead to our own mental agitation, guilt, remorse, and fear of revenge or punishment. However, investigating this precept asks us to look at killing other animals and even insects. Short of killing, we can also take this precept as advice against other forms of violence and physical harm. We can explore such areas as meat eating, euthanasia, capital punishment, abortion, killing or removing pests from our homes, and other forms of physical and mental injury wrought upon living beings. As with all the precepts, most meditators find that over time their awareness of and skill in working with non-killing and non-harming becomes progressively more refined and beneficial. The Buddha encourages us to rejoice happily in the knowledge that we are being skillful and not harming ourselves or others. Begin working with this precept by paying attention to any areas in your life where you harm yourself or other beings physically. When you are aware that you are causing harm how does it feel in your body? What is your state of mind? Do your actions cause worry, shame, guilt, remorse, or fear? How would you feel if your life was threatened?

2. **I undertake the training precept to refrain from taking what is not given.** Stealing stems from and strengthens our innate drive towards desire and greed. It agitates the mind and causes stress in the body of the one who steals. It

creates fear, worry, grief, and confusion in the victims. Beyond overt theft, here we are also asked to examine our relationship with material objects, possessions (ours and those of others), and the environment. There are many forms of taking what is not given: borrowing and never returning, taking office supplies from work, not correcting others' accounting errors when we are the beneficiaries of the oversight, wasting resources, consuming another's time needlessly, and hoarding beyond what we need. In examining this precept, we can explore mind states such as fear of not having enough, anger, envy, jealousy, self-sufficiency, generosity, relinquishment, and renunciation. Great opportunities for letting go abound when we skillfully practice this precept. Letting go of our attachments is an essential part of the practice of mindfulness and the path to awakening. To start working with this precept ask yourself how much you truly need in your life. How does it feel in the mind and body when you desire something that belongs to another? How do you feel after obtaining something that was not freely given to you? What are the long-term consequences of your actions? How have you felt after having your possessions taken from you?

3. **I undertake the training precept to refrain from sexual misconduct.** For many people sexuality is a unique and precious form of connecting with others that leads to joy and vitality. It can also be the source of much suffering. Many forms of harmful sexual conduct are obvious: adultery, incest, rape, coercive sex, exploitation, catcalls, sexual harassment, exhibitionism, and voyeurism. However there are many subtle forms of harm that occur through the power of our sexuality. For example flirtation often seems

harmless, but often there is an undercurrent of tension and stress. There can be uncertainty about each person's sincerity. Often the two persons involved in flirting have different purposes, intentions, and expectations. It can be unwelcomed by one person and a form of harassment. Other areas of sexuality that can be harmful are pornography, sexually suggestive advertising, sexually provocative media, sexist jokes and innuendos, sexually objectifying glances, and sexually enticing attire. In working with this precept, as with the others, we ask ourselves, "How can I live in this world in relationship with others without harming anyone and be the most helpful and beneficial?" Start working with this precept by noticing your relationship to sex. How do you feel when you think about sexuality? What do you notice in your body and mind when you notice that you are having sexual desire? What do your fantasies inform you about your relationship to sex? Do you detect any harm to yourself or others by your sexual conduct (i.e., thoughts, words, and actions)? How have you felt after being harmed sexually?

4. **I undertake the training precept to refrain from lying.** Our speech has a profound impact on ourselves and others. Communication between people assumes a level of accuracy and honesty. When we lie, even when we bend the truth a little, we increase the confusion and uncertainty in the world. It fosters distrust. In many of the Buddha's discourses he stressed the importance of telling the truth. Given the rapidity and prolific nature of written and spoken words in our modern world, speaking the truth is even more critical. Lies can destroy relationships, cause wars, result in legal actions, and cost valuable time, resources, and money.

There are many forms of unskillful speech, some overt and some very subtle: blatant lies, jokes based on untruths, fibs, lies by omission, gossip, chit-chat, idle chatter, abusive speech, profanity, and rumors. Many meditators find this precept to be very challenging and to require constant vigilance. You can start working with this precept by just noticing your intentions when speaking. Are they skillful or unskillful ones? Is there a theme of trying to appear a certain way to others? Do you need to speak so much? How does it feel in your mind and body when you tell a lie? How do your words impact others? How have you felt after being lied to?

5. **I undertake the training precept to refrain from intoxicating drinks and drugs that lead to heedlessness.** With the purpose of meditation being to wake up and to see things clearly as they actually are, the importance of this precept is obvious. Each meditator has to decide for himself or herself whether this means complete abstinence or moderation with alcohol or drugs. For some meditators, direct experience shows that any consumption of intoxicating substances distorts one's perceptions, results in unskillful action, speech, or thoughts, and should be avoided completely. To start working with this precept, notice what motivates you to want a drink or mood-altering substance. Before taking intoxicating substances do you find your experience of the present moment lacking or difficult? Do you treat yourself or others differently after having a drink or drug? How do you feel in the body and mind when you recollect your experience(s) of being intoxicated and heedless? How have you felt when you were around

someone who was intoxicated and was behaving unskillfully?

It is helpful in beginning to work with the 5 precepts to be realistic and to be kind to ourselves. It is common in the beginning of practice to become overwhelmed by the awareness of all the unskillful and injurious things we unconsciously do. We don't want the processes of investigation, insight, and change to strengthen the unskillful habits of self-loathing, compulsivity, self-denial, resentment, or neglect. These mind states can be counter-productive to meditation and cause one to give up. It is important to recognize that the precepts impact areas of our behavior that are deeply ingrained habit patterns. For most of us, changing our behavior takes time, diligence, and hard work. Meditators who embrace working with the precepts find the investment to be well worth the effort. Not only are our own lives positively impacted by our skillful actions but many others are as well. In practicing skillful ethical conduct, we give the world the gift of being harmless. Given all the violence, harm, confusion, stress, and suffering in the world, this particular gift is invaluable.

SKILLFUL LIVELIHOOD

"Generosity, kind words,
doing a good turn for others,
and treating all people alike:
these bonds of sympathy are to the world
what the linchpin is to the chariot wheel."

- Jataka 20

The Buddha also recognized that how we earn our living has a significant impact on our physical, mental, and spiritual well-being. Therefore, it is important to reflect on one's work in the world and whether it is skillful, beneficial, and promotes the well-being of others or whether it causes harm, discord, or confusion. Occupations that harm oneself, others, animals, or the environment or that are fraudulent, coercive, deceitful, unbeneficial to others, or that foster greed, hatred, or delusion are considered unskillful. Occupations that do not cause harm to ourselves or others and that are helpful are considered skillful. In addition, the Buddha described 5 specific forms of unskillful livelihood that should be avoided: dealing in weapons, living beings, meat production, producing or selling poisons and intoxicants. Some examples of jobs that may cause unintentional harm include: selling products by false claims, charging more than a fair profit in exchange for goods or services, exploiting clients who are desperate or in distress, gambling, and coercive or pressured sales measures. Frequently meditators experience a deepening connection with and satisfaction from their jobs as their meditation practice matures. Others find that their jobs no longer align with their deeper intentions for living and go on to find other means of support.

As part of developing a meditation practice and working with skillful livelihood it is important to examine several questions: How do you spend your time? What are your deepest intentions in this life? From where do you receive your support? What is the impact of your conduct in the world?

GENEROSITY AND RENUNCIATION

"If beings knew, as I know, the results of giving and sharing, they would not eat without having given, nor would the stain of selfishness overcome their minds. Even if it were their last bite, their last mouthful, they would not eat without having shared, if there were someone to receive their gift."

- *Iti 1.26*

Another important aspect of skillful ethical conduct is what the Buddha called **dana** (*Pali* for giving or generosity). He would often recommend this as the sole practice for people just starting out on the spiritual path. The practice of being generous helps us to become less attached to our possessions and to develop a deep appreciation of those with whom we share. It also gives us an opportunity to reflect on our relationships and our interdependency. Besides material goods (food, money, etc.) we can share our time and skills with others. Many meditators practice generosity in the form of service to others. This can involve volunteer work in local or global communities, teaching meditation, sharing the *dhamma*, and other forms of helping and supporting others in need. Sometimes just quietly and attentively listening to someone's concerns and experience can be a challenging opportunity to be generous. In a rapid-paced world where many people experience loneliness, alienation, and isolation, the gift of being heard is often greatly welcomed.

A special word on **renunciation** (*nekkhamma*): The practice of generosity requires renunciation and relinquishment. Whether it is time, energy, or resources, we need to renounce ownership of that which we give away. This can be accomplished on different levels: it can be a superficial renunciation of something that we do not cherish much and therefore is not that important to us. Or it can be a profound and intentional letting go of an item we deeply value. It can be done hastily or with careful reflection. It can also be done with the skillful intentions of benefiting the recipient while helping ourselves by cultivating the practice of letting go. Or it can be done without much care for the recipient and/or with self-loathing, self-denial, or self-punishment.

On a very deep level the core of the Buddhist path is about renunciation and letting go. The Buddha and his monks and nuns renounced their families, homes, and all possessions to pursue directly the practice that leads to liberation. They lived homeless and celibate lives and begged for their sustenance. Most of us at SIM are not monastics and have not renounced the world on that level. However, we can still practice deeply and use renunciation as a tool toward progress on the path. When we meditate, our practice is to continually let go of distraction, tension, and confusion and return to calm, clarity, and mindfulness. During practice we learn about our mental **defilements** (*kilesa*) and practice relinquishing them. The 3 root defilements are greed (*lobha*), hatred (*dosa*), and delusion (*moha*), which are often operating below our level of awareness. Combinations of these are the cause of all of our unskillful thoughts, words, and behaviors. They give rise to all of our suffering. The Buddhist path is about waking up to these defilements and then investigating, uprooting, and eliminating them. Ultimately the goal of practice is to let go of our attachment to everything.

To begin working with generosity and renunciation, investigate your relationship to your possessions (property, money, and belongings). Do you believe that you are attached or cling to your stuff? How do you feel in the body and mind when you notice clinging to your possessions? How does it feel when you let go of the clinging and/or give something away? What motivates you to give? How do you feel when you are the recipient of a gift?

ADDITIONAL PRACTICE SUPPORTS

"Greater in combat
Than a person who conquers
A thousand times a thousand people
Is the person who conquers herself."

- Dhp. 103

Before we address the actual meditation practice, we will look at other factors that aid us in developing the skill of meditative awareness. In addition to the skillful ethical conduct listed above, it is helpful to reflect on other areas of our lives. The way that we spend our time has an important impact on our mind and body (see "skillful intention" page 88). Like an athlete who is training for optimal performance, meditators need to optimize their conditions to make progress in meditation. In particular we need to exercise caution regarding where we place our **attention**. If we are doing a lot of multi-tasking, this can be detrimental to developing concentration. Frequently checking email, excessive web-surfing, or watching TV for hours can drain the mental energy needed for meditation and create a lot of mental chatter. Also, the type of sensory input we take in can have an impact on our state of mind. For example, violent or hateful media, pornography, and frivolous or trivial information can disturb the mind and waste our limited mental energy. This counters our purposes for having a meditation practice. Developing mindfulness tames a mind that is agitated, grasping, and confused and creates a mind that is calm, balanced, and wise. We then can greet whatever circumstance arises with wisdom and compassion.

"When faced with the vicissitudes of life,
one's mind remains unshaken,
sorrowless, stainless, secure;
this is the greatest welfare."

- SN 2.271

The Buddha taught a practice of **guarding sensory input**. There are two components to this sense restraint. The easier one is to avoid contacting objects that disturb our minds (e.g., that activate our latent greed, hatred, and delusion). We do this by simplifying our lives, reducing clutter, slowing down, and by abstaining from sights, sounds, etc. that prior experience has shown us lead to stress and suffering. In particular, hurrying and haste erodes one's mindfulness and should be reduced. The other, more difficult practice of safeguarding the sense doors involves letting go of sensory objects that trigger our defilements. We can learn to abandon the habitual reactivity of the mind that is triggered by certain experiences. We can develop a mind of equanimity that can weather any hardship and allow us to act skillfully regardless of external conditions. For example, if our boss or partner has a tendency to speak to us in ways that cause us to get angry, we can use mindfulness to see our reactivity, work towards relaxing the tension that comes with the reactivity, and eventually release it. We can remain in mental balance and respond to the conversation in a helpful way. It is possible to develop our minds to the point that we are no longer triggered towards anger or retaliation. We will have more to say about not clinging and equanimity later (see "Skillful Effort" page 29 and "Skillful Intention" page 88).

It is also important to take good physical care of ourselves. Proper nutrition without excessive quantities of food, sugar, fat, chemical additives, toxins, alcohol, or caffeine is helpful. Adequate sleep, periods of rest, and exercise (and/or yoga or Chi Gong) are also beneficial. Most meditators find that lifestyle decisions such as these come naturally with practice. As the power of our mindfulness grows, we develop a more refined discernment of what is beneficial and what is not. Many faulty strategies are dropped and more skillful ones adopted as we see ever more clearly better ways of living in this world.

In addition to the practices described in this book, most meditators need the support of other meditators. Given how contrary to mainstream culture *dhamma* practice can be, we need to support each other on the spiritual path. For many, an important part of practice is the "*kalyana mitta*", which is *Pali* for "spiritual friend." It is helpful to discuss our meditation practices, get tips and guidance, and share difficulties with other meditators. We can do this both with individuals and in the context of belonging to a **meditation community** such as SIM. As part of having *kalyana mittas* it is important to work with qualified and skillful meditation **teachers**. These are advanced practitioners who have had training to teach meditation and are part of a larger community of practitioners. SIM is affiliated with larger meditation communities that have many accessible teachers – the Insight Meditation Society in Barre, Massachusetts, the Spirit Rock Meditation Center in Woodacre, California, and the Insight Meditation Center of Redwood City. It is beneficial to have regular **practice interviews** with a meditation teacher. These can be conducted within the setting of a residential retreat or outside of retreat. Interviews of individuals or small groups of meditators are conducted by the teacher asking the meditation student(s) about their practice. Student and teacher work together to determine how to best support the student's meditation practice. Areas that the student finds difficult or that would benefit from additional instruction and practice are determined and an appropriate plan is agreed upon. The student may offer the teacher dana to express his or her gratitude and to take part in the system of mutual support between student and teacher that has thrived in Buddhism for 2500 years.

As our meditation practice deepens, we can unearth difficult memories, have uncomfortable, repetitive thought patterns, or periods of intense struggle. Usually the practice gives us ample tools to cope with and effectively process any difficulties that arise. Sometimes the help of a fellow meditator or teacher is sufficient to keep us on track. However, some meditators find that they need additional support in the form of **psychotherapy**. It may be beneficial to seek out help from a therapist who practices mindfulness and uses it in his or her counseling practice.

FAITH AND THE 3 REFUGES

"One should not chase after the past
nor place expectations on the future.
Rather with insight see into
each state as it arises in the moment."

- MN 133

Faith (*saddha*) is another skillful mental quality that supports meditation. Some meditators are initially averse to acknowledging this factor given its strong connection with organized religion. However, we need at least a little faith to begin practice. If you believe that there is no value in meditation, it is unlikely that you would be reading this. So we begin with the kernel of faith that there may be some benefit to meditation. As our practice grows and we begin to see the benefits of practice, faith in practice grows as well. For many practitioners, faith in their practice becomes quite strong and keeps the forward momentum of practice going during difficult periods. At some point in practice it is helpful to formally acknowledge one's faith by taking the **3 refuges** (*tisarana*). These are spoken formally as:

1. I go for refuge to the ***Buddha***.
2. I go for refuge to the ***Dhamma***.
3. I go for refuge to the ***Sangha***.

Most Westerners who take the refuges do not consider them as indicating a blind faith in a deity or a religious icon. Rather, we consider that the Buddha was a human being, like us, who was able to fully awaken. The Buddha taught us the *Dhamma* to help us awaken too. The teachings come down through the ages to us in the form of writings and an oral tradition. We can take refuge in the fact that the instructions are sufficient for our practice and that we have the capacity to follow them to the goal of liberation. "*Sangha*" was initially meant as the community of enlightened monks and nuns that lived at the time of the Buddha. In our times the term applies to the community of meditators and can include a group such as SIM or all of the Buddhist practitioners throughout the world. The key point with *Sangha* is that it is a community of mutual support and that we cannot do the work of awakening on our own. In taking the refuges we are trusting that by following the example and teachings of the Buddha, and with the support of the community, we can become liberated too.

2. TRAINING IN CONCENTRATION (MENTAL DEVELOPMENT) – (SKILLFUL EFFORT, MINDFULNESS, AND CONCENTRATION)

"I know of no single thing more conducive to great harm than an unrestrained and undeveloped mind.
I know of no single thing more conducive to great benefit than a restrained and developed mind."

- AN 4.45

With the first training in ethical conduct we are laying a wholesome foundation for stabilizing the mind. The second training in concentration involves calming and cultivating the mind in order to allow its innate wisdom to arise. In order to do this we must develop several related skills:

    a.   Skillful effort
    b.   Skillful mindfulness
    c.   Skillful concentration

As stated earlier, none of these trainings are very effective when practiced in isolation. It becomes apparent during practice how each skill aids the others and forms an integrated system for transformation. When the 3 trainings are each developed and practiced together we find a very powerful system for living.

SKILLFUL EFFORT

"Train yourself in doing good
that lasts and brings happiness.
Cultivate generosity, the life of peace,
and a mind of boundless love."

- Itivuttaka 1.22

Central to developing skillful effort is being able to discern what is skillful (*kusala*) from what is unskillful (*akusala*); What is wholesome and healthy and what is not? We must ask, "What causes harm to ourselves and others and what is beneficial and helpful?" This takes some reflection and is not always obvious. Many of us have long standing patterns of thoughts, speech, and action that cause gross or subtle harm. We can be so used to doing things a certain way that we do not see that our actions are unskillful. As our practice develops there is a refinement of what is skillful and what is not. Most practitioners have many areas in their life where greater clarity comes with practice. As change is implemented and new, more skillful patterns are established, we can see more clearly the harm we once were causing, and rejoice in the healthier patterns we are establishing. The Buddha described 4 specific ways to practice skillful effort:

1. **Prevent** new unskillful states from arising.
2. **Abandon** unskillful states that have already arisen.
3. **Develop** new skillful states.
4. **Maintain** and strengthen skillful states that have already arisen.

As mentioned earlier, we want to reflect on these practices before, during, and after any action we take be it mental, verbal, or physical. It is helpful to consider if one or more of the root defilements (greed, hatred, or delusion) are present. If we can be certain that they are all absent and that their opposites (generosity/renunciation, lovingkindness, and wisdom) are present, then it is skillful. Skillful effort provides balance to mindfulness. In developing mindfulness, we are strengthening the skill of accepting what is present in each moment. However, we need to look out for and not accept that which is unwholesome, harmful, or not useful. It is important in working with skillful effort to realize that we are human and will make many mistakes. We need to be gentle with and forgiving of ourselves and to realize that it takes time and work to develop these skills. The practice of lovingkindness (see page 90) can help us to accept our faults, let go of our guilt, and strengthen our stamina for further purifying our thoughts, speech, and behaviors.

SKILLFUL MINDFULNESS

"This is the direct path for the purification of beings, for the surmounting of sorrow and lamentation, for the disappearance of suffering and discontent, for acquiring the true method, for the realization of freedom...."

- *The Satipatthana sutta MN10*

Finally we come to training in meditation. This is the reason for which most people come to SIM. Earlier we gave the SIM definition of mindfulness: **moment-to-moment, non-judgmental awareness**. The Buddha had a more specific definition of **mindfulness** in terms of the qualities we bring to our attention. This definition of mindfulness is most clearly described in the *Satipatthana sutta* (the 4 foundations of mindfulness *sutta*), which is the historical basis of insight meditation practice. In the *sutta* the Buddha states that: 1) awareness should be diligent (meaning it should have deliberate intention and skillful effort); 2) awareness should have a clear comprehension and understanding of the objects of attention; 3) we should put aside our desire and aversion toward the objects of our meditation; 4) we should have awareness of both our internal and external experience; 5) we should notice the changing nature of experience (i.e., the arising and passing away of phenomena); 6) there should always be sufficient awareness to know that we are being mindful of the object; and 7) we should have awareness of objects while being independent from and not clinging to anything in the world. Although this sounds like a tall order, with practice many meditators are able to bring these qualities to their attention for sustained periods of time. Like any skill the more we practice mindfulness, the easier it gets and the more it becomes second nature. In our training in mindfulness we are creating new, healthy habits of mind and relinquishing old, unhealthy ones.

The Buddha also defined **mindfulness** in terms of 4 specific, important categories or objects of awareness:

1. **The body** (*kaya*).
2. **Feeling tone** (*vedana*).
3. **Mind states** (*citta*).
4. *Dhammas* – (mental objects or phenomena).

These are known as the **4 foundations of mindfulness** (*satipatthana*). We will now look at each one of the foundations in more detail. One caveat is that these instructions have been interpreted in myriad ways over the millennia since the time of the Buddha. What is presented here is the way that these instructions are interpreted and taught at SIM. A more detailed or comparative analysis of different mindfulness techniques is beyond the scope of this book.

THE BODY

"It is through this fathom-long body that one reaches the end of suffering."

- AN 4.45

The 1st foundation of mindfulness is central to practice. In fact, mindfulness meditation is called an embodied or **body-based practice**. Many of us have lived our lives trapped in the self-constructed prison of thoughts and concepts. We are shut off from awareness of our bodies. We can spend the whole day lost in thinking, unaware of mounting tension in our bodies. When we suddenly notice the mounting stress and pain it can be difficult to let it go and relax. Our culture is one that focuses on the external appearance and performance of the body while neglecting inner awareness and nurturing of the body. In many teachings the Buddha remarked that the entirety of our experience of the world is known only through the body, and specifically through what he called the **6 sense bases** (seeing, hearing, smelling, tasting, feeling, and thinking) and their corresponding 6 sense objects (sights, sounds, odors, flavors, touches, and thoughts). In meditation practice it is essential to develop mindfulness of these 6 senses (see page 62). We are cultivating the ability to be with our sensory experience without being lost in it, clinging to it, or pushing it away.

There is a wholesome, healing quality to developing body awareness. By paying attention in a relaxed, non-judging way to the sensations that arise and pass away in the body, we are giving ourselves a precious gift. We can notice areas of our body that are stressed and knotted up and then make a conscious effort to investigate and deconstruct them, release and relax the tension, and allow the body to be freer and more at ease. If we have injuries or chronic body issues such as chronic pain or fatigue, we can use non-critical awareness and investigation to develop a more wholesome and integrated relationship with our bodies. In meditation we learn the skill of accepting the conditions of the body and mind regardless of how difficult they may be. Mindfulness has a natural quality that softens, relaxes, and encourages the release of tension, discomfort, and stress. Most meditators find that practice with mindfulness of the body is well worth the investment and transforms their relationship with their bodies.

As we develop our *vipassana* practice and work with all 4 foundations of mindfulness we forge a direct experiential link between the different aspects of our being. The connections between the body, breath, emotions, and thoughts are an essential area of investigation in insight practice. By connecting our mental experience with our bodily experience we develop powerful skills for understanding ourselves, healing psychological problems, recovering from trauma, and relieving stress and suffering. Greater awareness of the body-mind connection develops an early warning system that allows us to notice physical and mental stress earlier and to make skillful choices about how to respond to the stressful situation, bringing the mind and body back into balance and calm. We are learning a more holistic way to live in the world, with greater awareness and acceptance of our inner and outer experience. This allows our natural qualities of wisdom and compassion to mature and inform our every thought, word, and action.

THE BREATH

*"Mindfulness of breathing when developed and cultivated
is of great fruit and benefit."*

- *MN 118*

The process of breathing is a vital function of the body. In fact, if we are deprived of our breath we will perish in a few minutes. In the practice of insight meditation the breath serves as an **anchor** of our attention. It is always present and functions as a stable foundation upon which we can develop our mindfulness and concentration. When the mind wanders the anchor gives it a base to which it can return. We use the anchor to train our awareness to stay in the present moment. When the attention is returned repeatedly to an anchor like the breath, we develop the skill of being able to intentionally focus the awareness on a single object for increasing periods of time without distraction. For most meditators the breath ideally suits this purpose. Breathing occurs automatically, yet we can also consciously control it. It is subtle, and we live our lives mostly unaware that we are constantly breathing. With practice of breath awareness, it becomes easily located and sensed. It is also constantly changing and serves as an optimal object with which to gain insight into the impermanence of experience. Increasing awareness of the breath naturally has a calming and concentrating effect. When the mind is steadily with the sensations of breathing, it is not with the distractions and concerns that usually occupy our thoughts and fritter away our days. The breath can become a refuge from the ravages of the unruly mind. Over time, with a committed practice, many meditators come to experience the breath as a beloved friend and trusted ally in their efforts to live joyfully, peacefully, and with a wise heart.

GUIDED MEDITATION I: THE BREATH

Begin your meditation period by finding a quiet location where you can be free of distractions and interruptions from other people, pets, bothersome noises, and electronic devices. It is helpful to have a silent timer with an alarm to set for the duration of your meditation period. We recommend starting with 15-20 minutes. Sit comfortably in a chair or on a cushion on the floor (see the figures in Appendix 2, page 110). If sitting in a chair, the feet should be in stable contact with the floor. In any seated position, the back should be straight with the head firmly balanced on the shoulders and the hands resting calmly on the legs or in the lap. The posture should be alert but relaxed. There should be no straining or struggle to stay upright and balanced. It is best to shut the eyes gently or if that is not comfortable then to have a soft gaze at a 45° angle. It is helpful at the beginning of the meditation period to set the intention to put aside our normal worries, plans, concerns, and memories. We want to dedicate our full attention to our experience of the present moment.

Start with general overall body awareness. Notice the sensations of the body sitting here right now. If it is hard to feel any sensations, you can focus on the contact of the feet with the floor or of the buttocks with the seat of the chair or cushion. After a few moments take a few slow, intentionally deeper breaths. Notice the sensations of the breath as it courses through the body on the inhale and relax and let go on the exhale. After several of these deeper breaths allow the breathing to return to its natural rhythm. Continue to follow the sensations of the breath coming into the body on the inhale and exiting the body on the exhale.

The training in mindfulness develops a profound, non-reactive awareness of our sensory experience. We are attempting to connect as deeply as possible with the raw sensations of our body moving with breathing and the sensations of moving air in contact with the body. Unlike some forms of yoga or pranayama breathing, we are not trying to control or manipulate the breath. We are also not trying to visualize the breath or conceptualize the breathing process. If being aware of the breath is uncomfortable or frightening, try to notice this reaction to the breath sensations and stay with them. If this is not possible, you can return your awareness to your body sitting.

Frequently, the mind will naturally drift off of the breath and wander to some sound, thought, memory, image, body sensation, or other object. This is a crucial moment of the meditation. Set the intention to wake up to the fact that you are no longer with the sensations of the breath and have drifted off. It is important not to get into a struggle with your attention or be angry with yourself for not staying with the breath. You can even develop some gratitude for noticing that you are no longer aware of the breath. Let go of whatever it is that caught your attention and, without analysis or dialogue, gently return the awareness to sensations of breathing. We need to do this process over and over as the mind stays with the breath for a while and then drifts off again and again. This is how we build our skills of mindfulness and concentration.

As the mind becomes more concentrated by stronger, more continual awareness of the breath sensations, move the awareness to the sensations of breathing where they are most strongly felt. For some people this will be the sensation of the breath as it enters the body through the nostrils. For others it will be the sensations of the rising and falling of the abdomen or chest during breathing. It is important to choose one of these locations and move the awareness to the sensations of inhalation and exhalation at that spot. You should stay with that location for the remainder of the meditation period. Some people find it helpful to use a silent and gentle mental note to help keep the awareness with the breath. This can be "in" and "out" for the nostril sensations or "rising" and "falling" for abdomen or chest sensations. This is an optional step and should not distract you from being experientially aware of the breath.

To connect more deeply with the sensations of breathing, you can investigate the different qualities of breath: fast vs. slow, long vs. short, smooth vs. irregular, warm vs. cool, and so on. This step is also optional and your investigation should not be too analytical or cause the mind to struggle or debate. Another useful practice with breath meditation is to relax any tension that is noticed in the process of breathing. It is okay to make small changes in the breath (i.e., slower, shorter, deeper, etc.) in order to make the breath more comfortable. This has a tendency of increasing one's ability to keep the attention on the breath. After an appropriate period of time (i.e., when the timer alarm sounds), end your meditation period by returning the awareness to the sensations of the whole body sitting. For a few moments notice the body and any differences from the start of the meditation period. When you are ready, open your eyes. It is helpful to reflect on the meditation period in terms of understanding and following the instructions and how you can improve your technique next meditation period. You can also reflect on any insight(s) that you had during the period. Some people keep a meditation journal to keep track of their meditation experience and insights. This is optional. You do not want to get lost in analysis, criticism, or debate. Before rising from your seat it is best to set the intention to maintain your meditative awareness by bringing the same quality of mindfulness to all of your activities. Also, you can set the intention to practice breath meditation again, either later the same day or tomorrow.

GUIDED MEDITATION II: THE BODY

Begin your meditation period by developing mindfulness of breath sensations as described in Guided Meditation I (page 37). After the mind has become stabilized on the breath for a period of time, open the awareness to body sensations. When a sensation in the body becomes more prominent in your awareness than the breath, you can intentionally move the awareness from the sensations of breathing to that body sensation. For example, while you are being mindful of the breath, if you noticed a pressure sensation in your knee, you would move your awareness to the sensation in the knee. Investigate the body sensation. Notice such features as location, size, depth, intensity, vibration, temperature, and/or clarity (diffuse vs. precise). As with breath awareness, investigating the qualities of body sensation is optional and should not be analytical or lead to excessive comparison or debate. The main point is to be aware of body sensations as objects of mindfulness. We are training the mind to be present with what is happening in our body in the present moment. Using silent labels helps connect with sensation. Some examples are: "sensation," "pressure," "dullness," "sharp," "warmth," etc. In the beginning it is best to avoid labels that are charged or that have hidden judgments such as "pain," "my injury," "loneliness," "frustration," etc. When the body sensation fades or becomes subtle, let go of it and intentionally return your awareness to the sensations of breathing. Stay with breath sensations for a while until another sensation in the body becomes prominent. In this way we use the breath as an anchor by stabilizing our attention on the breath and then intentionally moving it to prominent body sensations. As before, if you notice any tension building in the breath or body, you can make small adjustments to be more comfortable. It is best not to be constantly moving, fidgeting, or changing posture. After the meditation timer chimes, end the meditation period as before, returning awareness to the sensation of the whole body sitting. Before getting up, set the intention to leave the seated meditation period and proceed with mindfulness.

GUIDED MEDITATION III: THE BODY SCAN

Another useful practice of mindfulness of the body is the body scan. This is done by systematically moving the awareness through each part of the body noting what sensations are present. For each area of the body, the sensations are noted and the qualities of the sensations are investigated before moving on to the next body part. We can notice both sensations on the surface of the skin and also deeper inside the body. If tension or stress is noticed, it is released and relaxed. Although the body scan meditation is meant as an exercise in mindfulness and is not strictly a relaxation exercise, many people find it very relaxing. In fact for most meditators, the biggest challenge with the body scan is staying alert, mindful, and awake. Also, many meditators do not notice a lot of sensation when first learning the body scan. However with a little practice, most are amazed at how much sensation can be felt in the various parts of the body. This technique can strengthen body awareness and help us to more deeply inhabit our bodies. It is an excellent method for strengthening concentration.

The body scan is usually performed with the meditator lying on his or her back with the arms to the sides, legs relaxed out straight, and the eyes closed. It is best to be on a mat on the floor rather than in a bed or sofa, which may make it difficult to stay awake. You may want a pillow under the head and/or knees. It is also possible to do the body scan meditation while sitting in a chair or on a zafu. Begin by getting a general sense of your body lying down. Make any necessary adjustments to be comfortable for the meditation period. Take several intentionally deep breaths, releasing any tensions and relaxing on the exhales. After this, allow the breathing to find its natural rhythm. Although you can notice the sensations of breathing in this posture, the point of the body scan is to notice sensations throughout the body in a systematic way.

Start with the left foot. Notice any sensations in the toes of the left foot. You may not notice much at first. Whatever you notice is okay. That is what your experience of the body is in this moment. There is no need to move the foot or strain to feel sensations. There is no need to judge or analyze the experience. We want to bring to this exercise the same degree of kindness, presence, and patience that we have in all of our other mindfulness meditations. If the mind wanders away from the sensations of the body, gently and without judgment return the awareness to the part of the body being sensed. We need to do this over and over until the concentration builds and we can continually stay present with the body sensations. If you find that you are drowsy and falling asleep, you can take a few deep breaths to bring up the energy level of the mind. Other helpful techniques for waking up the mind: bring the knees and/or hands up so they have to be held in balance and/or open the eyes while looking softly at the ceiling. If all else fails, you can move to a chair or stand up for the rest of the body scan.

Next move the awareness from the toes to the sole of the left foot and feel what sensations are present. Shift the mindfulness to the left heel and notice any sensations. Cultivate a sense of curiosity and openness as you continue scanning through the rest of the body, section by section, for several seconds to a minute per section; left ankle, left lower leg and calf, left knee, left thigh and hip, right toes, right sole, right heel, right ankle, right lower leg and calf, right knee, right thigh and hip, pelvis, lower back, upper back, abdomen, chest, shoulders, left fingers and hand, left arm, right fingers and hand, right arm, neck, jaw, mouth, nose, area around the left eye, area around the right eye, left ear, right ear, forehead, back of scalp, and finally, the top of the head.

When you have slowly and mindfully scanned the entire body in this way, open the awareness to the whole body again. Spend a few moments noticing what is present in the body. Notice if there are any changes from when you began the body scan. Before ending the meditation period spend a moment reflecting on your experience of the body scan. Where you able to follow the instructions? Are there any clarifications that are needed? Set the intention to bring the mindfulness you developed during the scan to the next activities of your day. When you are ready, you can open your eyes and get up.

FEELING TONES

"Centered, mindful, alert,
the Buddha's disciple discerns feelings,
how feelings arise, where they cease,
and the path to their ending.

With the ending of feelings, one is free of want
And is liberated."

- *Iti 46*

The 2nd foundation of mindfulness is feeling tones. This does not refer to what we call in English "feelings," meaning emotions. Rather, feeling tones are the hedonic or affective tone of experience. For every moment of experience of the body or mind there is a feeling tone associated with it. Feeling tones are one of three types: pleasant, unpleasant, or neutral. For example, if we see a loved one smile, we may experience a pleasant feeling tone. If we stub our toe, usually the most immediate response is a feeling tone of unpleasant. Neutral is experienced when we do not have a pleasant or unpleasant feeling. Most of the time we are not aware of feeling tones. Usually feeling tones are present below our level or awareness. What we experience instead of the feeling tone is a reaction to it. The feeling tone is amplified into wanting more of the experience if it is pleasant (desire) or wanting to get rid of the experience if it is unpleasant (aversion). This reactivity is what causes our suffering (see "dependent origination" page 79). However, if we can learn to pay attention to the feeling tones themselves, we can develop a powerful tool for understanding how we experience the world and the relationships we form with that experience.   With that knowledge we can train ourselves to be less reactive and more at peace regardless of our circumstances.   This is a type of renunciation that is at the core of Buddhist practice.

GUIDED MEDITATION IV: FEELING TONES

Begin your meditation period by developing mindfulness of breath sensations as described in Guided Meditation I (page 37). Once the mind has some stability on breath sensations (after several minutes of the sitting period), open your awareness to feeling tones. For every experience of a body sensation, sound, thought, or emotion there will be an accompanying feeling tone: pleasant, unpleasant, or neutral. The practice here is to notice the feeling tone and not get caught in its story, in analysis, or in reactivity to the experience. At first it can be difficult to notice the feeling tone and often there are a lot of neutral feeling tones. We usually experience neutral as feeling nothing. Using the noting process can be helpful. A silent label of "pleasant," "unpleasant," or "neutral" helps train the mind to recognize the feeling tones. If the feeling tone changes, make a note of the shift in tone. For example, you may be aware of pleasant, then unpleasant, followed by neutral in rapid succession. As the feeling tones fade, return to the breath as the anchor of awareness. Continue the meditation by being mindful of the breath, shifting awareness to body sensations and/or feeling tones as they arise, are noticed, and then pass away. At the end of the meditation period, move the awareness to the breath and then the whole body for a few moments before you open your eyes.

MIND STATES

"All experience is preceded by mind,
Led by mind,
Made by mind.

Speak or act with a corrupted mind,
And suffering follows
As a wagon wheel follows the hoof of the ox.

Speak or act with a peaceful mind,
And happiness follows
Like a never-departing shadow."

- *Dhp 1-2*

The third foundation of mindfulness is mind states. The
Buddha defined these in specific ways: the presence or absence
of greed, hatred, and delusion. At SIM we teach this foundation
as mindfulness of thoughts and emotions. Either practice is
beneficial. Our ordinary experience is to be carried away by
our mental states. In any given moment we can get lost in the
memory of an interaction, rehearse a future dialogue, have a
fantasy, get caught up in some strong emotion, or cogitate on
some problem in our life. This is most often done without
mindfulness and below the level of our awareness. For most of
us an endless stream of mental chatter occurs almost every
waking moment. There can be a ruminative and limiting nature
to our mental states. What we think and feel is a result of and
forms further habits of mind. There is a repetitive nature to our
mental patterns. Unfortunately, due to a lack of mindfulness,

many of our mental states are influenced by the root defilements of greed, hatred, and delusion and result in unskillful speech and behaviors.

As we develop meditative awareness, we want to develop present moment awareness and to know when we have become lost in our thoughts and emotions. We do this by connecting our mind states to sensations in the breath and body, and to feeling tones. For example, when we are caught in an emotionally charged mind state or find that we are lost in a train of thoughts, we can recognize this, pause, and move our awareness from the thought(s) to sensations in the breath and body. We can notice what feeling tone is present. As always, we do not want to get lost in analysis or discursive reasoning. Rather than creating a struggle with your thinking and feelings develop a friendly, curious, and accepting attitude. We want to keep our inquiry on the simple level of asking the question, "What do I feel in the breath and the body when I am having this thought or emotion? What is the feeling tone associated with it?" Then drop the content or story line of your mind and focus on how the process of thinking and feeling manifests in the body. This transforms the abstract concepts of the mind into the direct visceral experience of the moment. The propensity of the mind to constantly proliferate ideas (called papanca in *Pali*) is derailed by mindfulness. With practice, the mind can become calm and focused. The power of a concentrated mind can be used to skillfully solve problems and generate insights.

Ultimately, working with mindfulness of the mind states trains us to be continuously present in the moment and not perpetually lost in thoughts and emotions. When we get caught up in stressful mental chatter, we can recognize that our attention has been hijacked and we can return the mind to a state of peace, balance, and clarity. Using skillful effort (page 29) we prevent and abandon unskillful states of mind and develop and maintain skillful ones. Although this may seem a daunting task, with practice, it can become second nature.

GUIDED MEDITATION V: MIND STATES

Start the meditation period as you have done previously by stabilizing the awareness on the breath for several minutes (see page 37). Then open the awareness to thoughts and emotions. Often these accompany each other, with emotions triggering thoughts and vice versa. Do not to stay in the content of your thoughts and emotions; rather be aware that you are thinking and/or having an emotion. Drop the story of the thought or emotion and investigate how it manifests in the breath and body. Notice what sensations are in the breath and body. Where are they felt? Is there a feeling tone associated with the thought or emotion? You can use subtle silent labels such as "thinking" or "emotion." You can be more specific with labels such as "memory," "planning," "judging," "image," "joy," "anger," "sadness," etc. If you find yourself getting lost in the thoughts and emotions, or in the noting, gently return the awareness to the breath. If you continue to have repetitive thoughts or emotions that are creating tension or distress, some other labels that help to let go are: "it's just a thought," "it's just an emotion," "not now," "letting go," or "it's okay." When a thought or emotion fades, return to the anchor of the awareness (the breath). As before, intentionally and repeatedly shift your awareness between the breath and other prominent aspects of your experience. Take your time with each object, knowing it as fully as possible without lapsing into judgment, concept, or analysis. After the meditation timer chimes, end your session as usual.

DHAMMAS

"Just as the ocean has a single taste — that of salt — in the same way, the dhamma-vinaya has a single taste: that of freedom."

- *Ud 5.5*

The fourth foundation of mindfulness is what the Buddha called "*dhammas.*" This can be translated into English as "phenomena," "mental factors," or "categories of experience." *Dhammas* are specific lists of skillful and unskillful factors of mind and body that, when developed wisely, can lead to awakening. Perhaps more so than the others, this foundation of mindfulness takes a high degree of skill and diligent practice to investigate and develop. Early in practice it is helpful to know what the factors of the *dhammas* are, but working with them can lead to analysis and discursive thinking. As practice develops, the mind is trained to recognize and work with the fourth foundation. Many meditators find working with *dhammas* a powerful tool for cultivating the mind to be free from suffering.

TABLE 2: *DHAMMAS*

The Five Hindrances (*panca-nivarana*)

> Sensual desire (*kamachanda*)
> Ill-will (*vyapada*)
> Sloth and torpor (*thina-middha*)
> Restlessness and worry (*uddhacca-kukkucca*)
> Doubt (*vicikiccha*)

The Five Aggregates of Clinging
(*panca-upadanakkhandha*)

> Form (*rupa*)
> Feeling tone (*vedana*)
> Perception (*sanna*)
> Mental formations (*sankhara*)
> Consciousness (*vinnana*)

The Six Internal and External Sense-Bases
(*cha-salayatana*)

> Eyes and visual objects
> Ears and sounds
> Nose and smells
> Tongue and tastes
> Body and tangible objects
> Mind and mental objects

The Seven Factors of Awakening (*satta-bojjhanga*)

> Mindfulness (*sati*)
> Investigation of states (*dhammavicaya*)

Energy (*viriya*)
Joy (*piti*)
Calm (*passaddhi*)
Concentration (*samadhi*)
Equanimity (*upekkha*)

The Four Noble Truths (*cattari-ariya-saccani*)

The truth of suffering (*dukkha*)
The origin of suffering (*dukkha-samudaya*)
The cessation of suffering (*dukkha-nirodha*)
The path leading to the cessation of suffering (*dukkha-nirodha-gamini-patipada*):

The Noble Eightfold Path
(*ariya-atthangikamagga*):
Skillful View (*samma ditthi*)
Skillful Intention (*samma sankappa*)
Skillful Speech (*samma vaca*)
Skillful Action (*samma kammanta*)
Skillful Livelihood (*samma ajiva*)
Skillful Effort (*samma vayama*)
Skillful Mindfulness (*samma sati*)
Skillful Concentration (*samma samadhi*)

THE 5 HINDRANCES

These are unskillful mental factors that stem from the 3 root defilements of greed, hatred, and delusion. They hinder the mind from being mindful and concentrated. Like all phenomena they are impermanent but can derail the meditation process. The hardest part of working with the hindrances can be recognizing when they are present. They often operate below our level of awareness but influence our thoughts, speech, and action in unskillful ways. Our first task regarding the hindrances is to be mindful of them. Rather than getting into a struggle to suppress or eliminate them, we need to take our time in seeing them clearly and investigating them in terms of the 4 foundations of mindfulness (i.e., breath, body, feeling tones, thoughts, emotions, etc.). One helpful approach is the **RAIN** formula: We **Recognize** the hindrance, **Accept** it, **Investigate** it, and **Non-attach** to it (e.g., don't identify with it as being "me" or "mine"). Using the noting process can be helpful (i.e., "this is desire" or "ill-will is present," etc.). Now we will look at each hindrance in more detail and give some specific tools to work with them.

Sensual desire manifests as wanting something that is pleasing to our 6 senses. It has an aspect of leaning into experience, wanting more of it. Types of sensual desire include wanting, lust, greed, envy, jealousy, addiction, and gluttony. Specific antidotes for working with sensual desire are: seeing into the nature of desire, understanding the negative consequences of it (not just its illusive attractive features), reflecting on the undesirable features of the object of desire, guarding the senses, renunciation, and generosity.

Ill-will is present when we do not want to be with our experience. It has a quality of recoiling from or pushing away what is present. Some forms of ill-will are: aversion, fear, hatred, anger, rage, annoyance, boredom, and resentment. Specific antidotes for working with ill-will are: developing lovingkindness, developing concentration, investigating the harmful effects of aversion, and finding gratitude for one's practice and one's good nature.

Sloth and torpor is a state of mind that has little interest in what is present. It can include dullness, heaviness, sleepiness, boredom, laziness, and lethargy. This can be due to physical fatigue but often is mental. When it is overwhelmed, frightened, or unable to cope with what is happening, the mind can disengage and check out. In working with this hindrance it is important to bring up more energy in the mind and body. The meditator can sit up straighter, take some deep breaths, breath cool, fresh air, open the eyes, stand up, splash cold water on the face, go for a walk, engage the practice more deeply, resolve to wake up, develop concentration by breath counting, bring the awareness out to the whole body, arouse energy in the mind by investigating what is present, and engage the cognitive aspect of the mind by reflecting on the teachings. If all this fails take a brief nap, but be cautious of making it a habit!

Restlessness and worry result when the mind is overactive. Concentration is poor as the mind darts here and there caught up in concerns and problem solving. Remorse over unskillful actions can also trigger restlessness and worry. Like the previous hindrance, it can be physical or mental or both. Specific techniques to work with this hindrance include: taking intentionally slower and deeper breaths, increasing concentration by breath counting, reflecting on the cause of restlessness and worry (i.e., worry over the future or remorse over the past), calming the mind with some lovingkindness, practicing walking meditation, and/or resolving to sit still and be mindful.

Doubt results when the mind is confused. We may be unsure of our practice or of meditation in general. Forms of doubt include uncertainty, resistance, murkiness, indecision, and inability to commit. Perhaps more than the other hindrances, doubt can derail the meditation process and lead the meditator to quit practice altogether. Therefore we have to be vigilant in order to recognize it, and to be committed to working skillfully with it. Self-doubt is rampant in our society and can be amplified in the early stages of practice. It is helpful to recognize self-doubt and the negative self-talk that accompanies it as just thoughts. They do not have to be believed or taken seriously and can be let go of. All thoughts are impermanent and will dissipate. Doubt will always fade away.

There is a role for discernment or skillful doubt in practice. Rather than blindly accepting the teachings or a teacher, the Buddha recommended that we practice and see the truth for ourselves. He recommended using discernment and the wise counsel of other practitioners to determine if a practice or teaching results in harm to ourselves or others. If it causes harm, it should be abandoned. If it is non-harming and beneficial it should be pursued. Some antidotes to doubt are studying the *dhamma*, reflecting on the teachings, discussing one's doubts with a teacher, reflecting on one's good qualities, acknowledging one's faith in practice, and taking (or re-taking) the 3 refuges.

THE 5 AGGREGATES OF CLINGING

The Buddha described the 5 aggregates as components or subdivisions of our physical-mental being. The mind has a tendency to consider these elements as self or belonging to the self. Clinging to them results in our suffering. Our task in working with the aggregates is to recognize them as aggregates and to investigate them through the discerning lens of the 3 characteristics: That is, to understand them as impermanent, a source of suffering, and not belonging to self (see page 85). **Form,** the first aggregate, is all of the physical matter in the world – the body and the objects that are experienced by the body. The remaining four aggregates are mental factors. The **feeling tone** is the affective tone of experience (i.e., pleasant, unpleasant, or neutral. See page 46). **Perception** is the way we characterize our experience with concepts and labels. For example we see a dog and our mind recognizes it as a dog and not a cat or a tree due to the faculty of perceiving. With the label of "dog" comes a variety of conditioned associations (i.e., animal, non-human, alive, cute, potentially dangerous, etc.). **Mental formations** are intentions and their results that are fabricated by the mind. Due to our conditioning, we have mental habits that shape the way each experience is processed and acted upon. Behaviors (thoughts, speech, and actions) resulting from our habits (mental formations) create further habits. This is how we shape and in turn are shaped by our experience (see "*kamma*" page 83). **Consciousness** is the awareness that arises in the mind when the 6 sense organs contact their respective sense object. For example, in seeing a dog, the eyes contact the visual image of the dog resulting in the arising of consciousness of the dog in the mind.

To begin working with the aggregates, start to notice that your experience can be deconstructed into these 5 elements. Also, notice how the mind clings to these 5 categories and tries to make them lasting, pleasing, and part of or belonging to the self. When you are aware of this process, see if you can let go of the clinging and just be with the raw experience of the aggregates. You can use mental noting such as "This is not me. This is not who I am. This is not mine." You can deconstruct the experience using the 4 foundations of mindfulness (How is it experienced in the breath, body, feeling tone, mind, and *dhammas*?)

THE SIX SENSE-BASES

The sense bases were described by the Buddha as the "all." What he meant was that all that we can experience and know involves one or more of the sense-bases. Each sense base has an internal (within the body) and an external (outside the body) component. The 6 internal and external bases are: the eyes and visual objects; the ears and sounds; the nose and smells; the tongue and tastes; the body and tangible objects; and the mind and mental objects. Like the 5 aggregates, the 6 sense bases are another way to categorize our experience and another way that we cling to that experience. In working with the sense bases it is important to begin to be mindful of when we are having an experience through a particular sense base, to see if clinging is present, to investigate the experience using the 4 foundations of mindfulness, and then to let go of the clinging. For example, hearing one of your old favorite songs may trigger nostalgic memories and you may feel sad. You would be mindful that you are having an experience through the sense base of the ears and sounds. You would see that sadness is present and open your mindfulness to the sensations of the breath and the body. You would do the same with the other foundations (feeling tones, mind states, and *dhammas*) to investigate what is present. You would see that the sadness is a form of clinging. Without judgment you would release the sadness and keep your mindfulness on the sound and hearing. You can use a silent note of "hearing." Working with mindfulness of the six sense bases in this way can be a rich area of investigation.

THE 7 FACTORS OF AWAKENING

These are factors that incline the mind towards concentration and mindfulness. Cultivating the 7 factors of awakening balances and develops the mind to receive the insights that are necessary for awakening. They are natural qualities of the mind that get obscured by the hindrances. Our task is to notice them and develop them further. Just putting our attention on the factors has a tendency to increase them. Skillfully working with the hindrances also benefits the arising of the awakening factors. Mindfulness has a tendency to weaken the hindrances and strengthen the awakening factors. As practice develops the awakening factors become an integral part of daily practice. The factors incrementally aid each other and balance each other. They can be viewed as a spiral staircase or a 7-spoke wheel. The full development of the 7 factors of awakening leads enlightenment.

Mindfulness, which was discussed in detail earlier, is an essential factor for recognizing and building the other factors. **Investigation of states** is a quality of mind that is curious and manifests as interest in the object(s) of meditation. **Energy** is necessary to keep the mind alert and skillfully efforting. **Joy** enlivens the mind and creates a relaxed connection to experience. **Calm** keeps the mind from becoming over-stimulated and aids in focus. **Concentration** is the quality of staying with the object(s) of awareness without distraction and one-pointedness of mind. **Equanimity** is the balance of mind that allows us to see into the true nature of things without attachment. The equanimous mind neither grasps at nor rejects whatever is present.

The **4 noble truths** will be discussed in the "Skillful View" section (page 76.)

GUIDED MEDITATION VI: *DHAMMAS*

Begin the meditation session using the instructions for mindfulness of breathing. (see page 37). When the attention has been stabilized on the breath for a few minutes, open the awareness up to all of your experience. When an object arises in your field of awareness, be it body sensations, sounds, feeling tones, or mind states simply notice it. As objects of mindfulness, these experiences are noted as well as their relationships with each other. For example, when investigating a sensation in the body, notice the sensation, its relationship (if any) to the breath, any associated feeling tones, and any thoughts or emotions related to the sensation. You can use the labeling process. If the mind gets too attached to the experience, becomes lost in analysis, or drifts aimlessly, return the awareness to the anchor of the breath.

When investigating *dhammas*, begin by noticing if one or more of the *dhammas* are present. For example you can ask, "Is there sensual desire (a hindrance) present?" or "What aggregate is noticed now and what does clinging to it feel like in the body?" or "Is there clinging to one of the senses and where is that felt in the breath? What is the feeling tone?" or "Is there an awakening factor present (i.e., mindfulness, joy, calm etc.)?" As skill in working with *dhammas* increases, the breath and body will help you determine what factors are present. For example, if the breath is rapid and shallow and the body is tense, there may be a hindrance such as ill-will present or there may be clinging to a sight. If the breath and body are relaxed and at ease, factors such as joy and calm may be present. As you work more with these factors they become more apparent. As your practice develops you can also work with the other *dhammas* (i.e., the 5 aggregates, 6 sense bases, 7 factors of awakening, and the 4 noble truths.) Ultimately the goal is to experience all phenomena through the understanding of the 4 noble truths. During meditation, if the mind is struggling with determining which factors are present, return the awareness to the sensations of breathing. When the meditation session is over, end as usual (see page 37).

GUIDED MEDITATION VII: INSIGHT MEDITATION

The practice of insight meditation (vipassana) involves being mindful of the entirety of one's experience. When we open our awareness to all that is present in a non-biased way, it is called choiceless awareness. To practice choiceless awareness meditation, combine the instructions already given for each of the 4 foundations of mindfulness. After settling the awareness on the breath for a few moments, open to the entirety of your experience. Notice each object of awareness as it arises, is present for a while, and then passes away. Ideally, each object is noticed and released without preference. It can be helpful to use a gentle mental note of each object. For example, in practicing choiceless awareness one might have noting like this: "breath," "sound," "memory," "breath," "pleasant feeling," "desire," "warmth," "fear," "planning," "sound," "pressure," "breath," etc. It is helpful to end the meditation session as usual by opening the awareness to the whole body and then setting the intention to bring mindfulness into the next activities of the day.

GUIDED MEDITATION VIII: WALKING MEDITATION

The Buddha described four standard postures in which one can practice meditation: walking, standing, sitting, and lying down. In addition to formal sitting meditation practice, many people benefit from walking meditation. This is a formal practice where mindfulness is brought to the act of walking. This can be done any time we are walking and is especially useful if there is a regular period during the day when one walks (i.e., during the commute to work). It can also be practiced as part of one's daily meditation practice.

To begin, find an area of level ground of about 20 paces where you can walk back and forth. As with the sitting meditation, during walking meditation you want to create conditions that will optimize your ability to be mindful. For your walking path do not choose a path with a lot of distractions or traffic. Walking back and forth is better than strolling, which can lead you to be distracted by all the sights and sounds that you encounter. Start at one end of the path. Begin by closing the eyes and placing the attention on the body standing. Notice if there is any tension or holding and see if you can release it and relax. Create an alert but relaxed posture. Allow the breath to find a natural rhythm and depth. During walking meditation, instead of using the breath as the anchor of your awareness, use the sensations of the legs moving or the contact of the bottoms of the feet with the ground. Before walking, set the intention to be mindful of the physical sensations of walking. Begin walking. Notice the sensations of walking in the legs and/or feet. As with breath meditation, when the mind wanders notice that it has left the object of meditation, and without agitation or regret, gently return the awareness to the sensations of walking. The training in mindfulness is to bring the attention back to the anchor over and over again. The gaze is best kept at a 45° angle down toward the ground. The hands can be folded in front or back or released at the sides. When you get to the end of the path pause briefly, reconnect with body sensations, turn around, and walk back the length of the path. Continue the walking meditation for a period of 15-20 minutes to start. You can use a timer to keep track of the period. As with sitting meditation, when you are finished walking set the intention to bring the mindfulness you have just developed into the next activities of your life.

SKILLFUL CONCENTRATION

"There are these roots of trees and empty huts. Meditate, do not delay lest you regret it later."

-MN 19

Concentration is a quality of the mind whereby it is able to focus on and stay with an object of awareness without distraction. This can be any object such as a visual object, a mantra, or the breath. Lovingkindness (see "Skillful Intention," page 88) and the body scan meditations can also be used as concentration practices. Concentration allows us to connect more deeply with what is present. Concentration and mindfulness are complementary to each other and synergistic. Each is necessary for the cultivation of the other. At SIM we sometimes teach breath concentration practice. This is done by focusing the awareness on the sensations of breathing to the exclusion of all other objects. All other body sensations, sounds, thoughts, etc. are let go of and the attention is continually brought back to the breath. When this is done repeatedly concentration builds and one is able to stay with the breath for longer and longer periods. Eventually, intrusive thoughts drop away and the mind becomes steadily focused on the breath. Often the highly concentrated mind will experience states of peace, serenity, and bliss. For some meditators, high levels of concentration lead to the meditative absorptions (*jhanas*). These are temporary states of consciousness where the mind is unified and external stimuli is faintly noticed or absent. In the discourses the Buddha often speaks of the *jhanas* and their central role in skillful concentration. There is controversy regarding the *jhanas* with modern meditation teachers. Most agree that the role of concentration in meditation is not solely to reside in blissful states. Rather, concentration is used to settle the mind, allowing the wisdom of insight to blossom. If one wishes to pursue deep levels of concentration, usually an extended period of practice (i.e., a residential retreat of one to several months) and a teacher skilled in *jhana* practice are required.

GUIDED MEDITATION IX: BREATH CONCENTRATION

It is important to find a comfortable and stable posture when doing concentration practice. Typically one sits for longer sessions (i.e., 1-2 hours or more) without getting up and with little or no physical movement. Many meditators find sitting in a chair to be optimal for these longer periods. It is helpful to have a quiet space, free from distractions or interruptions. Begin the sitting meditation in the usual manner (see page 37). Focus the awareness on the sensations of the breath to the exclusion of all other objects. Relaxation is essential to concentration practice. The mind needs to be alert, but relaxed. Most meditators who practice breath concentration find it preferable to pay attention to the sensations of the breath at the nostrils rather than the chest or abdomen. When the mind wanders, gently bring it back to the breath. When you discover that the attention has strayed from the breath, it is crucial that you return the awareness with kindness and ease. Any struggle with the technique, will counter the concentration process. The art of concentration involves continually letting go of tension and stress and opening to joy and calm. For deep concentration to develop, all 5 hindrances must be abandoned.

Quiet mental noting of the breath can be helpful (i.e., "in" and "out"). Alternatively, counting can be used to keep the mind focused on the breath. To do this, silently note "1" on the 1st exhale, "2" on the 2nd exhale, etc. up to 9. Then count backward from 9 to 1 on the exhales and begin again from 1. When the mind wanders and you lose count, start over from 1. It is important to keep the counting subtle (in the background) with the majority of the focus on the sensations of the breath. As the mind becomes more concentrated, it is able to stay with the counting for long periods of time. Eventually the counting will need to be dropped allowing the mind to concentrate more fully on the breath. The breath may get very shallow and subtle. It may even seem to disappear. Try to stay with the sensations and continue to relax fully into being with the breath. When the meditation period is over, end as usual.

3. TRAINING IN WISDOM (SKILLFUL VIEW AND INTENTION)

"Thoroughly understanding the dhamma
and freed from longing through insight,
the wise one rid of all desire
is calm as a pool unstirred by water".

- Itivuttaka 91

The last of the three trainings, wisdom, is both the starting place and the culmination of the path. We need some initial wisdom to want to begin practice and to know how to proceed. As we practice the Buddha's path to liberation, wisdom builds and we become more skillful in life. Although developing mindfulness and concentration are essential steps on the path to awakening, they are not enough on their own. We need to use all of the path factors to generate wisdom. In this context, wisdom does not mean merely accumulated knowledge or a keen intellectual capacity. In Buddhism wisdom implies a deep understanding of and insight into the reality of existence. The 'insight' of insight meditation is an intuitive, non-conceptual seeing into the true nature of phenomena. It is a profound knowing of how things really are. Our ordinary minds are under the constant spell of ignorance – the opposite of wisdom. Due to this ignorance, we constantly misinterpret our experience, projecting onto it our desires, fears, and confusion. We engage in unskillful acts and create suffering for ourselves and others. In meditation practice we are constantly training to uproot ignorance by developing wisdom. We start with conceptual knowledge of the *dhamma* and, using the 3 trainings, develop it into insight. Awakening it is said, requires the full penetration of and profound insight into the 4 noble truths. When this is accomplished, wisdom is complete and the practitioner is awakened.

During practice we can have 2 types of insights: the personal and the universal. At the beginning of practice most of our insights are into our own personal psychological experience. These are aspects of our history and personality that relate to our suffering. They are often about our stories and are centered on the content of our experience (i.e., "**I** am an angry person," "**My** childhood was traumatic," "**I** am cruel to **my** partner," or "There is a lot of suffering in **my** life"). This is an important stage of meditative maturation. It is essential to see our habit patterns and areas of unskillful thoughts, speech, and actions and to begin working with them. Over time we can relax long-held tension patterns that have led to much suffering in our lives and create equanimity towards our past. We can forgive ourselves and others for the harm we experienced. Working with personal insights can help us live more skillfully, harmoniously, and peacefully. As practice develops, often our insights become less about our own personal experience and more related to universal experience. Insights at this level are not about our own personal stories but about the impersonal processes of interdependency (see "dependent origination," page 79) and the universal characteristics of life (see "Insight into the 3 characteristics," page 85). These types of insights are very profound and are at the heart of insight meditation. They are essential to awakening.

SKILLFUL VIEW

> *"When you know for yourselves that, 'These qualities are skillful; these qualities are blameless; these qualities are praised by the wise; these qualities, when adopted & carried out, lead to welfare and to happiness' — then you should enter and remain in them."*

  - AN 3.65

The training in wisdom has 2 components: skillful view and skillful intentions. Skillful view was defined by the Buddha as understanding the **4 noble truths** and understanding *kamma* (*karma* in Sanskrit). The Buddha refers not only to an intellectual understanding of the 4 noble truths, but a profound insight into and an experientially-based realization of the 4 noble truths. When that understanding is fully integrated into one's being awakening occurs.

THE 4 NOBLE TRUTHS

"Just as the footprints of all animals are encompassed by the footprint of the elephant, and the elephant's footprint is reckoned the foremost among them in terms of size; in the same way, all skillful qualities are gathered under the four noble truths."

-MN 28

The 4 noble truths are part of the 4th foundation of mindfulness and constitute the heart of the Buddhist teaching. The Buddha said that it was his discovery of the 4 truths that led to his awakening. The truths are not meant as a Buddhist dictum but are a fundamental insight into the way things actually are. Rather than focusing on metaphysical questions, the Buddha addresses the very practical issue of "what is the basic problem with life and how can it be rectified?" He does this in the traditional Indian medical format of making a diagnosis (1st truth), describing the cause (2nd truth), giving the prognosis (3rd truth), and prescribing the treatment (4th truth). Taken as a whole, the 4 noble truths give a complete picture of practice and encompass the whole dharma. Each truth is not just to be understood, but has a task that must be undertaken in order to penetrate the truth fully.

The 1st Noble Truth is the truth of *dukkha*. This truth states that inherent to life is *dukkha*. This Pali word is usually defined in English as "**suffering**." However, many people enjoy lives of privilege and do not believe they suffer. What *dukkha* points to in our lives is a baseline unsatisfactoriness that arises in response to our experience. The truth of *dukkha* is that we are constantly subject to stress and dissatisfaction. Though it can be subtle, much of the time we are not fully content with things as they are. The Buddha further defined this truth in terms of specific aspects of life: Birth, aging, death, sorrow, lamentation, pain, distress, despair, not getting what we want, having to endure what we don't want, and separation from people and things we cherish are all forms of suffering. He further defined suffering as the **5 aggregates of clinging** (see "the 5 aggregates," page 60). We cling to these 5 elements of our physical-mental experience. The task of the 1st noble truth is to **understand** the truth of suffering and to see the various forms of suffering in our lives.

The 2nd Noble Truth is the truth of the origin of *dukkha*. The Buddha stated that it is due to craving (*tanha*) that our suffering arises. It is our craving for and clinging to experience that causes us to suffer. There are 3 types of craving: 1) craving for sensual gratification (*kama-tanha*); 2) craving for existence (*bhava-tanha*); and craving for non-existence (*vibhava-tanha*). Examples of the first one are the craving we have for pleasure at the 6 senses (i.e., pleasing sights, sounds, thoughts, etc.). Craving for existence includes craving for types of experiences, meditative states, identities (i.e., spouse, parent, wealthy, famous, etc.), and the drive to continue living. Craving for non-existence includes wanting to die, craving for our suffering to end, wanting to numb out with intoxicants (or food, media, relationships, etc.), wanting our current experience to end, and craving to not be who we are.

At the core of understanding this truth is the crucial Buddhist concept of conditionality. Simply stated, all phenomena have causes and conditions. Everything we experience occurs in dependence on other factors. Although this seems obvious, it has profound implications for practice. If we can understand the causes and conditions of our suffering and stress, we can work to change these causes and conditions and eliminate suffering. A key aspect to this is the understanding that when we act unskillfully we create conditions that lead to our suffering and that of others. When we act skillfully, we benefit ourselves and others and we do not contribute to suffering. Eliminating the causes of suffering leads to its cessation.

The Buddha described a more detailed analysis of the origin of suffering by the process of **dependent origination** (*paticca-samuppada*, sometimes called "the cycle of reactivity" at SIM). Although a detailed analysis of this model is beyond the scope of this book, we will discuss it in general terms: Due to our ignorance of the 4 noble truths we live in this world and function based on habitual patterns of mind and body. When we encounter some experience using our 6 senses, we do so from this conditioning. Each encounter results in a feeling tone (pleasant, unpleasant, or neutral). We often react to the feeling tone with craving in the form of desire toward pleasant experience and aversion from unpleasant experience. We tend to ignore neutral feeling tones. If this reactivity intensifies, which it often does, we cling to the experience by forming an attachment to it. Usually we want more of the pleasant and less of the unpleasant. We experience agitation, stress, and suffering if we don't get our way.

The next stage of intensification of reactivity results in developing an identity around the experience. With identification we experience our attachment as personal. "This is happening to **me**." "Why can't I have it **my** way?" "You never listen to **me**." or "**I** don't like this." These are common internal dialogues signifying that we are caught in the process of dependent origination. By identifying with our experience, our habitual mind states contract around the experience. Our sense of who we are, our beliefs, our reasoning, and our intentions all contract too. This leads to unskillful thoughts, speech, and action, resulting in suffering. Unfortunately, dependent origination does not end with the suffering, but usually continues as further rounds of reactivity are triggered in a vicious cycle. We are continually trapped in this process of reactivity, unaware of its devastating nature, as we trudge from one experience to the next. Some Buddhists believe that the process of dependent origination affects us over many lifetimes, is shaped by our *kamma*, and produces further *kamma* for us.

Understanding dependent origination gives us a powerful tool to work with our suffering. There are many stages of our reactivity where we can intervene. By practicing the 3 trainings, we can replace ignorance with wisdom and unskillful habitual patterns with skillful ones. We can notice feeling tones as the first reaction in the mind after contacting an experience. We can note the feeling tone and investigate it in terms of the 4 foundations of mindfulness. It is especially useful to investigate how the feeling tone manifests in the breath and body. Connecting breath and body sensations to the feeling tones has a tendency to short circuit our reactivity. We can notice the urge of the feeling tone to intensify into craving. Practice helps us to abandon craving and not act on the urge to intensify. As soon as we recognize that we are involved in clinging and identification we can abandon them. We can choose to refrain from unskillful actions and cultivate skillful ones. As with all of practice, it is best not to struggle as we work with dependent origination or be harsh with ourselves for falling into the trap of *dukkha* again and again. It is healthier to have a curious, patient, and calm approach to practice. When we wake up and act skillfully, it is beneficial to rejoice, be happy with our success, and to take delight in the wholesome states we create. The task of the 2nd noble truth is to **abandon** the origin of suffering, craving.

The 3rd Noble Truth is the truth of the cessation of *dukkha*. This is the good news of Buddhism. There is a way out of our suffering and it is by abandoning the craving and clinging which is the source of our suffering. We can do this on a moment by moment basis by letting go of clinging when we see it. This needs to be practiced both during formal sitting meditation and in our daily life activities. As our skill in practice develops, more and more subtle forms of clinging are identified and abandoned. When the 3 trainings are developed to their fullest, awakening occurs. The Buddha called this "*nibbana*" which means "unbinding" (of clinging). It is the complete extinguishment of the flames of greed, hatred, and delusion. Other synonyms for *nibbana* are enlightenment, awakening, liberation, and freedom. The task of the 3rd noble truth is to **realize** the cessation of suffering. It is to realize *nibbana*.

The 4th Noble Truth is the truth of the path of practice leading to the cessation of *dukkha*. This is the **Noble Eightfold Path** (the 3 trainings). We begin our journey to awakening with an inkling of hope for relief from our suffering and a kernel of faith that the *Dhamma* describes a successful strategy to this goal. We gain initial wisdom from the words of others who have navigated the path before us. They teach us that there is a worthy goal, awakening, and the path of practice to reach it, the 3 trainings. Setting the intention for non-harming, we begin to practice diligently. The hard work of uprooting our harmful habits and purifying our conduct (speech, actions, and livelihoods) yields ample fruits along the way to sustain our practice. Our work with skillful effort helps us to discern what is harmful and what is beneficial. We continually strive to abandon the former and promote the latter. The mind is formally cultivated by training in mindfulness and concentration. A settled, developed mind produces insights into our experience. Through insight, we gain intuitive wisdom to refine our practice. Through hard work, we ultimately achieve penetrating wisdom and reach the end of our path – the end of suffering. The Buddha and generations of enlightened men and women after him, show us that it is possible in this very life. The task of the 4th noble truth is to **develop** the noble eightfold path.

KAMMA

"Beings are owners of their actions, heirs of their actions;
they originate from their actions, are bound to their
actions, have their actions as their refuge. It is action that
distinguishes beings as inferior and superior."

- MN 135

The Buddha also described skillful view as understanding *kamma* (*karma* in Sanskrit). Traditionally *kamma* is described as the moral law of the universe. We are all the owners of our actions. If we commit harmful acts to ourselves or others we shall, at a later time, reap unpleasant results from those actions. If we commit skillful ones we will reap favorable results. According to the Buddhist view, this cycle can occur within our lifetime or a later life. This view, which is a commonly accepted one in Asia where Buddhism began, has it that the *kamma* we produce and the *kamma* results we experience are caught up in *samsara*, an endless cycle of birth and death (and suffering). Buddhist tradition believes that there is no divine agent driving *kamma* and that there is no beginning of samsara. The goal of practice, many believe, is to get off this samsaric wheel of suffering. Some Western practitioners have difficulty believing in this world view. There has been debate in Western Buddhist circles as to whether belief in *kamma* is necessary for practice. In many discourses of the Buddha he says that it is. Each practitioner needs to determine for themselves how they want to relate to this aspect of the teachings.

"Intention, I tell you, is kamma. Intending, one does kamma by way of body, speech, and mind."

-AN 6.63

Intention is the essential piece in working with *kamma*. As the above famous quote signifies, the most important thing we can do is set skillful intentions. Regardless of the outcome of our actions, our intentions are paramount. According to the Buddhist view on intention, even if we kill someone accidentally, if our true intentions were wholesome, then we would not incur negative *kamma* and would not be blamable. In understanding the workings of *kamma* in our own lives, sometimes it is easy to see the unpleasant results from our unwholesome actions. Other times the results of our actions are not apparent to us. We can continue creating suffering for long periods of our lives unaware of the cumulative harm of our conduct. Sometimes we consciously or unconsciously cover over an unskillful intention with a skillful one. For example, we may be dishonest with someone, telling ourselves that they cannot handle the truth, when the real reason for our deception was to satisfy our own desire. Often our true motives have to do with building up our own image and sense of self (e.g., not wanting to look foolish or inadequate in front of others). The progressive nature of *Dhamma* practice helps us see deeply into our behaviors and their underlying motivations. We can use that wisdom to set ourselves free.

INSIGHT INTO THE 3 CHARACTERISTICS

"'All created things are impermanent'
'All created things are suffering'
'All things are not-self'
Seeing this with insight,
One becomes disenchanted with suffering.
This is the path to purity."

-Dhp 277-279

Another aspect of skillful view is seeing the 3 characteristics of existence (*tilakkhana*). As stated succinctly in the quote above, the Buddha taught that there are 3 aspects to our existence that we usually fail to notice. First, all of our experience is constantly changing. Nothing is permanent or eternal. Second, it is due to this change that we suffer. In a constant sea of change we find our lives unstable and unsatisfactory. We may get what we want or avoid that which we don't want, but it never lasts. We continually strive to arrange the conditions of our lives in particular, comforting ways. It is an arduous and endless task. Last, all things are not-self. That is, no matter how hard we look at our experience – our bodies, minds, and surroundings – we cannot find anything that comprises an enduring, unchanging self that we can completely master and control. None of the 5 aggregates of clinging (see page 60) can accurately be considered "mine", "who I am", or "my self." The 3rd characteristic of not-self is one of the most difficult Buddhist concepts to grasp intellectually. The Buddha refused to answer the question of whether or not there is a self or soul. Rather, he continued to point out the fact that when we construct a sense of self or act as if we have a self or soul, we suffer. As we practice the 3 trainings these key insights become more and more apparent and integrated into the psyche. Awareness of and skillfully working with insights allows us to let go of our resistance to the way things are and accept the true order of the world. This leads us home to being free from suffering. Central to the process of liberation is the relinquishment of the belief in the self as a permanent, discrete entity:

"...An enlightened one with the ending, fading out, cessation, renunciation, and relinquishment of all construing, all excogitation, all I-making and mine-making and obsession with conceit — is, through lack of clinging, liberated."

-MN 72

DHAMMA STUDY

"In whatever way they conceive (of self), the fact is ever other than that."

- MN113:21

Part of constructing wisdom on the path is *dhamma* study. We need to inform our practice by laying the intellectual foundations upon which the intuitive insights will develop. Available forms of study include dharma talks (live or recorded and distributed on the internet), books, journals, websites, and even movies. For many practitioners, the study of the *Pali suttas* is invaluable. These are considered the oldest complete record of the Buddha's teachings. There are many excellent English translations of the *suttas* in existence. One can start with reading a single *sutta*, a thematic anthology of *suttas*, and/or take a live or online *sutta* study class. A brief guide to *sutta* study is available from this author. Residential study retreats are beneficial and are becoming more available. It is helpful to dedicate a portion of time each day to studying the *Dhamma* and then integrating what is learned into one's meditation practice. See the "Additional Resources" (page 116) for suggestions for further study.

SKILLFUL INTENTION

"Whatever one frequently thinks and ponders, that will become the inclination of the mind."

-MN 19

The final factor of the noble eightfold path is skillful intentions. In the section on *kamma* we noted that our intentions are the most important aspect of our physical, verbal, and mental actions. The Buddha described intentions (thoughts) as either skillful or unskillful (wholesome or unwholesome). He noted that his thoughts/intentions could be categorized as 3 types. The 3 corresponding sets of unskillful and skillful intentions are:

Unskillful Intentions	Skillful Intentions
Desire, greed, lust	Non-desire (generosity/renunciation)
Ill-will, anger, hate, fear	Non-ill-will (lovingkindness)
Harmfulness, cruelty	Non-harmfulness (compassion)

For each of these pairs, we need to discern for ourselves when our thoughts are skillful and when they are unskillful. With skillful effort (page 29), we wish to cultivate the skillful thoughts/intentions and abandon the unskillful ones. Using the 4 foundations of mindfulness to investigate the 3 sets of intentions helps us to discern the wholesome from the unwholesome. When we are caught up in greed or desire, we can recognize that it is unskillful. We investigate the sensations of the breath and body, the feeling tones and mind states, etc.

Then we intentionally abandon the unskillful thoughts. Next, we cultivate the opposite. We cultivate the skillful intentions of generosity and renunciation. With ill-will, we can see when we are angry, hostile, fearful or otherwise resisting what is present. We let it go and cultivate lovingkindness (*metta*). When we are lost in thoughts of harmfulness such as wanting to hurt ourselves or someone else, say something cruel or unkind, or lash out in some way, we can release those intentions and cultivate compassion for ourselves and others.

It is helpful to practice cultivating skillful intentions as part of our daily practice. As the quote at the beginning of this section indicates, we influence the inclinations of our minds by the contents of our thoughts. Modern neuroscience and psychology have shown that habitual thinking patterns reinforce themselves. Neurological pathways are strengthened by continued use. Non-used neural pathways atrophy. We become what we think. Therefore it is important to be aware of the content of our thoughts and cultivate our minds skillfully for the good of ourselves and others.

LOVINGKINDNESS (*METTA*)

"Searching all directions with one's awareness,
one finds no one dearer than oneself.
In the same way, others are fiercely dear to themselves.
So one should not hurt others if one loves oneself."

- *Ud 5.1*

The Buddha taught **lovingkindness** meditation as a formal practice. *Metta* is the mind's and heart's inclination toward good-will. It is the bodily sensations, feeling tones, thoughts, and emotions that accompany our heartfelt wish for well-being, happiness, and freedom from suffering for ourselves and others. Its opposite is ill-will. For many meditators this practice is an important complement to their mindfulness practice. At SIM we encourage meditators to develop a daily metta practice. This opens the heart to accept the present moment no matter how difficult it may be and balances the wisdom gained through mindfulness. The practice of metta involves holding the thoughts or images of various persons in our hearts and wishing them well. We silently say certain phrases wishing lovingkindness. Beyond the words, we are cultivating positive feelings toward ourselves and others. We always practice lovingkindness for ourselves first, and then move to other persons. The traditional order is given in the lovingkindness guided meditation.

Lovingkindness is the 1st of the **4 *brahmaviharas*** (*Pali* for *divine abodes* or immeasurable qualities). These are beneficial, positive mind states that can be intentionally developed. A regular practice of cultivating them helps replace unskillful habits of mind with skillful ones. The 4 *brahmaviharas* are:

1. Lovingkindness (*metta*)
2. Compassion (*karuna*)
3. Sympathetic joy (*mudita*)
4. Equanimity (*upekkha*)

Compassion is the skillful response of the heart when it encounters suffering – ours or another's. Coming from a place of wisdom, the compassionate heart wants suffering to end and the being suffering to be happy and well. The opposite of compassion is cruelty. Sympathetic joy arises when we take unselfish delight in another's joy, well-being, and prosperity. The opposite of sympathetic joy is envy. Equanimity is the ability of the mind to stay balanced and non-attached regardless of the circumstances. The mind is stable, even in the face of pleasure or pain. The opposites of equanimity are desire or aversion. As meditation practice develops, the innate mind and heart qualities of the *brahmaviharas* also grow. However, like all aspects of the training, it is wise to cultivate them intentionally and regularly. Over time they become the natural inclination of the mind.

GUIDED MEDITATION X: LOVINGKINDNESS

When doing metta meditation, it is important to be comfortable and to make an effort to let go of concerns and internal quarrels. The posture should be relaxed and alert. Start meditating as usual with closing the eyes, moving the awareness to the whole body for a while, followed by a few minutes of meditating on the sensations of the breath (see page 37). Next, form an image of or have a general sense of yourself. This can be you at this point in time or an earlier one, including childhood and infancy. Wish yourself goodwill and lovingkindness. Say internally, slowly, the following (or your own similar phrases):

1. May I be safe.
2. May I be happy.
3. May I be healthy.
4. May I be free from suffering.

Repeat the phrases several times, pausing between them. Focus on any sensations in the heart area. Try to connect with any bodily sensations, feeling tones, and/or emotions present. Metta is not a dry intellectual exercise or one of rote recitation but an exploration of the visceral aspect of our wholesome connection to ourselves and others. If your mind wanders from metta gently return to the phrases. Try to avoid investigating, analyzing, or reflecting on any thoughts that arise. With metta practice we want to strengthen the connection to the pre-verbal, emotive parts of the mind.

After you have practiced metta for yourself for a while, let go of the image of yourself. Next bring to mind a benefactor or mentor - someone in your life who has shown you great kindness and concern. Get a sense or image of them in your heart area. Say the above phrases for them substituting "you" for "I" and connecting with the visceral aspects of your experience as above. After repeating these phrases and noticing the feelings of lovingkindness for several moments, let go of the impression you have of them. Continue lovingkindness for the following: a dear friend or loved one, a neutral person (someone you know casually), and a difficult person. Don't choose the most difficult person(s) in your life, just a mildly difficult one to begin with. Finally, practice metta for all beings everywhere (including yourself). When you end the lovingkindness meditation, you can continue with insight meditation or end your session by setting the intention to carry lovingkindness into all of your activities.

BUDDHISM

*"Both formerly and now, monks, I declare only suffering
and the cessation of suffering."*

-MN22

Buddhism is considered one of the world's major religions. By
some estimates over 300 million people throughout the world
consider themselves Buddhists. In many Asian countries where
Buddhism is the major religion, the types of Buddhist practices
observed look very different from those described in this book.
In these countries, many Buddhists consider the Buddha a deity
or at least a super-human. Accordingly, some Buddhist
scriptures depict a detailed and fantastical Buddhist cosmology
which is based on the law of *kamma*. There are human, animal,
heaven, hell, and other realms where beings are reborn
according to the results of *kamma* generated in previous lives.
Kamma that is generated in one's current life in turn influences
one's rebirth in the next life. This is the wheel of *samsara* and
the Buddha said that no first beginning to it can be found.
There is no central agent or god driving it. This view frames
spiritual practice as paramount to escaping from samsara and
the intention toward wholesome states as the ideal. The Buddha
discouraged devotional practice (e.g., praying to gods, chanting,
worshiping idols, and making offerings such as burning incense,
etc.) because these rituals often lead to clinging. They can
become hollow forms that have nothing to do with the 3
trainings and uprooting our defilements. However throughout
the millennia, these devotional practices have become central to
many Buddhist communities. Western Buddhists often practice
meditation for its positive benefits and its holistic ethical

framework while preferring to set aside the mythological, cosmological, and devotional aspects of Buddhism. Others embrace these views and practices. As this ancient Eastern religion takes root in the West, it is adopting the beliefs, inclinations, and practices of its host countries. It has particularly taken on shades of secularism, pluralism, materialism, and individualism. Modern psychology theory and practice is also a strong influence. It is an exciting time to be a Buddhist. There are numerous Buddhist practices and flavors of Buddhism available. Many offer skillful means for spiritual growth, and some can lead us away from our goals. For each of us who decides to embrace the *Dhamma*, whether we consider ourselves Buddhists or not, it is important to reflect often on our intentions and their results. Not that we want to obsessively scrutinize or criticize our meditation. Rather, using the skills gained through practice, we can develop an inner intuitive wisdom that will serve us through the worst (and best) of times. As the Buddha enjoins us, "come see for yourself."

MEDITATION RETREATS

After one has been meditating for a while it is helpful to invest in a more intensive period of practice. For most meditators attending meditation retreats periodically is an important complement to their daily meditation practice. Daylong meditation retreats are offered monthly in Sacramento at SIM and allow the practitioner to practice diverse aspects of meditation while delving deeper into practice. The format used is one of alternating periods of sitting and walking meditation. Instructions and discussions are usually offered. In addition, special topics and study daylongs are offered and are beneficial. The most concentrated form of practice occurs on residential meditation retreats. These range from a few days to a month or longer. Retreats are held at retreat centers such as the Spirit Rock Meditation Center (see "Additional Resources," page 116). On retreat, practice begins early in the morning and concludes in the late evening. Instructions, dharma talks, and meditation interviews are offered. Usually sitting and walking meditation periods are alternated. The retreat is held in silence, which creates a container for going deeper inside and developing strong mindfulness and concentration. Often retreat centers charge for and provide room and board. Sometimes the retreat is offered on a *dana* basis. In the vipassana tradition most teachers do not charge a fee for their teachings. Usually they are supported by *dana* received from students. This practice allows the student to express their gratitude for the teachings in a tangible way. SIM offers an annual residential meditation retreat that is popular. The retreat experience is a precious opportunity to practice intensively in an ideal setting.

MEDITATION COURSES

Live or online meditation courses can be useful means to learn the skills required to practice meditation. They can offer support for starting or further developing a daily meditation practice. SIM offers a beginning meditation course that is very popular and has graduated over 700 meditators in 9 years. The course consists of weekly evening sessions for 6 weeks and a daylong meditation retreat. Over the course, each of the 4 foundations of mindfulness are introduced and practiced with successively. During each class there is an opportunity for group meditation practice, a question and answer session, a lecture of the week's topic, and an introduction to the daily meditation practice homework. A course syllabus is provided and the course instructors share their meditation experiences in a frank and helpful way. Lovingkindness (*metta*) meditation and practice supports such as the 5 precepts are introduced as well. Most find the daylong retreat to be particularly valuable. Many students have found the SIM introduction to meditation course to be worthwhile and some, including the author, have taken the course multiple times. In addition to taking a meditation course in person, there are increasing opportunities to learn meditation through online meditation courses. This form of practice allows the student to have support for beginning a meditation practice from the convenience of their own home and on their own schedule. Online courses offer the student a correspondence with an experienced meditation instructor or an option to "audit" the course by following the didactic materials and practicing meditation on one's own. See "Online/Correspondence Courses," page 117 for a list of courses.

RECOMMENDATIONS FOR STARTING A MEDITATION PRACTICE

"You yourself must strive;
the enlightened ones only point the way.
Those who follow the path and meditate
will be freed from the bonds of Mara."

-Dhp 276

If you have decided to take up meditation and start a practice you will want to optimize conditions to give yourself the best chance for success. Given the busyness our modern lives, with all the distractions that we encounter daily, embarking on a meditation practice can be challenging. The following are some suggestions that many meditators have found helpful. These suggestions are successive and incremental and need not be pursued all at once.

1. Commit to a time period to try a **regular meditation practice** (i.e., 1 or 6   months). Set the intention to apply effort to succeed.
2. **Discuss** it with your partner, friends, or family to get their support.
3. Consider taking **the 3 refuges** and following **the 5 training precepts** during this period.
4. Dedicate a **daily period** of time for sitting meditation. Some people have to give up some other activity to do this (i.e., waking up earlier, less time on the computer or watching TV).

5. Set up an area of **your home** for sitting meditation. Some people have an altar with a statue of the Buddha, pictures of loved ones, or other symbolic items. Most important is to have a place that you will be relatively undisturbed.

6. Use a **silent timer** with an alarm for your sitting periods.

7. Start with 15 -20 minutes sitting meditation daily and over time, increase by 5 minute intervals.

8. Using the **guided meditation instructions** in this book, start with breath meditation (see page 37) for the first week and each week incrementally incorporate the other instructions.

9. **Commit** to working with the instructions for the full meditation period and resist impulses to end the session early or get up to attend to some other task.

10. Begin and/or end each period of sitting meditation with a few moments of **lovingkindness (metta) meditation**.

11. Set the intention to practice **mindfulness in daily life**. Using a reminder timer such as the invisible clock (www.invisibleclock.com), sticky notes with mindful reminders, or regularly timed mindfulness breaks throughout the day can be helpful.

12. If you have walking as part of your daily routine, try doing it practicing **walking meditation** or spend some time on formal walking meditation practice.

13. **Study** the dharma by reading and/or listening to dharma talks (see "Additional Resources" page 116).

14. Reflect on the teachings and how they apply to your life.

15. Attend a **meditation group** such as SIM.

16. **Discuss** your meditation practice with other meditators.

17. Take the SIM Beginning **Meditation Course** or an online course.
18. Attend a **daylong meditation retreat**.
19. Attend a **residential retreat** for several days such as the SIM annual retreat or a retreat center such as Spirit Rock.
20. Find a qualified **meditation teacher** to further guide your practice.
21. At the end of your committed practice period, **assess** if meditation has been a beneficial practice for you.
22. If your practice is beneficial, continue to practice.

CONCLUSION

"I say to you: All conditioned things are subject to decay. Practice diligently."

-DN16

Insight meditation practice aims to cultivate meditative awareness in all aspects of one's life. Mindfulness is systematically practiced using the Buddha's teachings on the 4 foundations of mindfulness: the body, feeling tones, the mind, and *dhammas*. Although mindfulness is essential to awakening, it is not sufficient. In order to reach the goal of the Buddha's teachings (e.g., the cessation of suffering), one has to gain wisdom through insight. This is accomplished by the development of the 3 trainings: ethical conduct, concentration, and wisdom. We practice the 3 trainings by developing the noble eightfold path: skillful view, skillful intention, skillful speech, skillful action, skillful livelihood, skillful effort, skillful mindfulness, and skillful concentration. As practice matures, each of these skills becomes progressively refined and our way of being in the world becomes more and more skillful, more and more wholesome. When we stop harming ourselves and others, suffering diminishes. The insights we gain through practice allow us to see deeply into our existence and the nature of life. We come to understand on a visceral, intuitive level that all we experience is constantly in flux, is inherently unsatisfactory, and cannot be considered a self or what belongs to self. Our ignorance of and resistance to these 3 characteristics of experience is the cause of our suffering. By letting go of clinging, freedom comes. Awakening is the complete abandoning of all clinging. It is possible in this life.

This concludes our overview of the practices and teachings at SIM. I hope these pages have been helpful. I encourage you to put down this book now and pick up the practices. See if meditation and the supports discussed are beneficial in your life. The Buddha recommended that rather than blindly following his or anyone else's teachings, you validate your experience with your own inner wisdom. Try out the *Dhamma*. If you feel up to the challenge of the effort required to become free, take your place among the countless meditators over the last 2500 years who have followed the Buddha's teachings all the way to awakening. What do you have to lose?

APPENDIX 1: QUESTIONS AND ANSWERS

The following are questions commonly asked by students in the SIM Beginning Meditation course: [Listed are a few possible answers to these questions.]

Question: How do I stop thinking when I meditate?
Answer: The vast majority of meditators are not able to stop the thinking process during meditation. Thinking is what our minds do. It is best not to get into a struggle with your thoughts. We recommend giving yourself permission to think. Thinking is made an object of meditation like all other aspects of our experience. Rather than getting lost in the content of the thoughts, it is best to notice when there is thinking happening. You can use a subtle label such as "thinking" or "It is just a thought," and investigate the thought using the 4 foundations of mindfulness (i.e., Where is the thought felt in the body and breath? What is the feeling tone? Are there associated emotions? Are any hindrances present?). Alternatively, you can allow thoughts to stay in the background of your awareness while you are mindful of the breath in the foreground.

Q: Can I use my heartbeat as an object of meditation?
A: It is generally not recommended to focus on the sensations of one's beating heart as an object of meditation. There are several reasons for this: a) the sensations of the heart beating can be quite subtle and difficult for many people to follow; b) the heart beat is a rapidly moving object, which makes it difficult to concentrate upon; and c) for some people, paying attention to the heartbeat can cause anxiety and agitation.

Q: I have trouble feeling my breath. What can I do?

A: Many people report initially having trouble noticing the sensations of breathing. However, often after a little practice, they can feel the breath without difficulty. A few tricks to get started are: a) begin each session with a few deeper, deliberate breaths and notice where in the body the breath is felt the strongest. Stay with that location as the breath settles into its normal rhythm. If the sensations are lost, then take a few more deep breaths to amplify the sensations; b) put your hand on your chest or abdomen to feel the rising and falling sensations; and/or c) visualize a balloon expanding and contracting in your chest or abdomen with each in and out breath. Feel the sensations of the balloon moving. As you can connect more directly with the breath sensations, drop the image of the balloon.

Q: Is it alright if I listen to music while I meditate?
A: We recommend that the formal sitting meditation be practiced in a quiet space without music or other external distractions. Music in particular creates many associations in the mind and can be counterproductive to insight meditation.

Q: Can I light a candle, burn incense, ring a bell, or bow to an image of the Buddha before I meditate?
A: Some people find joy in observing these practices before or after their formal sitting meditation. Doing them can be helpful in setting a positive mood, strengthening faith, or feeling gratitude for one's practice. If you choose to do these devotional practices, caution must be exercised to prevent them from overshadowing the meditation process or becoming objects or rituals that you cling to. We recommend occasionally putting them aside and meditating without observing the practices at least some of the time.

Q: I have heard that some forms of meditation use visualization of energy, gods, clouds, animals, etc. Can I use visualization while I am meditating?

A: Many of us have the habit of mind of overlaying visual images, concepts, ideas, and associations onto our experience. In insight meditation we are attempting to see through these overlays and be with our experience directly. For that reason we do not recommend visualization exercises in insight meditation.

Q: Do you have any suggestions for a racing mind?

A: It is common for people to struggle with their minds and to have many thoughts when they start to meditate. Some suggestions are: 1) begin each meditation session setting the intention to put aside the thoughts, plans, and memories for the duration of the meditation period; 2) keep the attention on the breath by using silent, subtle labels such as "in" and "out" or "rising" and "falling;" 3) when the mind wanders into thinking and you recognize it, use a subtle label such as "thinking." Gently and with kindness toward yourself, return the attention to the breath; 4) if the mind is wandering a lot sometimes it helps the concentration process to count breaths (see page 71); and 5) recognize that a racing mind is often the hindrance of restlessness and worry and use the recommendations given in the 5 Hindrances section (page 56).

Q: I find that when I meditate I get very calm and start drifting off to sleep. What can I do?

A: This is also a very common scenario for meditators. Many of us are sleep deprived. Some people need better quality and quantity of sleep in their lives more than they need meditation.

It is very difficult to cultivate meditative awareness if we are fatigued and weary. Despite getting adequate sleep many meditators still find their minds are sluggish and sleepy during meditation. This is known as the hindrance of sloth and torpor. Some skillful techniques for working with this hindrance are: a) take a few intentionally deeper breaths; b) open the eyes, looking gently down at the floor to let in more light; c) stand up; d) practice walking meditation; and e) if all else fails, take a brief nap and then return to meditation. See the section on the hindrances for more recommendations (page 56).

Q: I would like to start a meditation practice but I can never find the time. What can I do?

A: The development of meditative awareness in most people's lives results in profound changes in priorities, meaning, and quality of life. Like any skill, it requires patience and practice. Many people find that they have to intentionally set aside time each day to practice. It is best if this is done consistently and with commitment. Often meditating first thing in the morning after waking up is beneficial. This can bring calm and purpose to the rest of the activities of the day. When starting a meditation practice, often we need to let go of some of our other activities or time commitments. We can find areas in our lives that are less beneficial or even counterproductive to our greater goals in life. Examples are excessive time on the internet, checking emails, watching TV, consuming other types of media, gossiping, or talking too much. Eliminating or reducing these activities often gives people plenty of time to practice. As our meditation practice builds, we find that time spent meditating is invaluable and that it actually creates the conditions in our lives whereby we spend more time focusing on what is truly important.

Q: I've been practicing faithfully for several months and things in my mind seem worse now than ever. I don't think I am meant to meditate. What should I do?

A: For many people starting a meditation practice can stir things up in their lives. When the practice is successful, we see into our old habit patterns and begin to realize all the ways that we harm ourselves and others. During this stage of practice, it is common to perceive that meditation is adding to our suffering and to feel that we are not cut out for meditation. It is important to take the insights we gain about our reactivity and unskillfulness and transform them into positive change. When things get rough in practice, it is helpful to be easy on ourselves, practice lovingkindness, discuss our difficulties with our meditation friends (*kalyana mittas*) and teachers, study the dharma, and keep practicing.

Q: The more I sit, the more pain I experience in my body. I thought meditation was supposed to help ease pain and relax tensions. What can I do?

A: This is a common experience. Chronic muscle tension often causes numbness in the nerves. As the meditation process progresses and the muscles relax, many people start to feel new areas of pain and tension. In unraveling the knots of our minds and bodies sometimes we experience new unpleasant sensations. Since the stress and tension developed over years and decades, patience with the meditation process is important. Almost everyone who continues with meditation experiences lasting relief of tension, reduced pain, and greater ease in the mind and body. Lovingkindness and good self-care are helpful during the process. Some meditators find it useful to exercise or stretch before and after sitting meditation. Some practice forms of mindful movement such as yoga or Chi Gong.

Q: Do I have to sit perfectly still while I am meditating?
A: No. In the beginning of one's practice, it is important to regularly check in with the posture and adjust it to optimize conditions that favor mindfulness (i.e., a straight spine that is relaxed but alert) and to keep the body comfortable. As one's practice grows, many meditators find that it aids concentration and mindfulness to sit still with little movement. During practice it is helpful to try the exercise of not moving during an itch. Often we reflexively, without awareness, scratch itches or otherwise make endless, unconscious adjustments to our posture based on sensations of pleasure and pain. When we sit through an itch without moving, carefully paying attention to what is present in the mind and body, a rich area of investigation opens up. In addition to the many physical sensations, we can observe feeling tones and the reactivity of the mind. It is also a great exercise to observe impermanence. The sensations of the itch and the mind states resulting from them always change and eventually fade away.

Q: When I practice metta meditation I don't feel anything. What is supposed to happen?
A: The practice of lovingkindness (*metta*) meditation is meant to produce in the heart and mind intentions of good will toward ourselves and others. This can involve speaking the *metta* phrases, holding visual images in the mind, and noticing bodily sensations, feeling tones, and wholesome thoughts and emotions. Frequently when one begins the practice of *metta*, no feelings or sensations are noticed. One can find the practice of reciting the phrases by rote dull or difficult. It is important to

be patient and to try to bring up a felt-sense of the subjects of metta in your heart area. Some people benefit by looking at a picture of a loved one or of themselves as a small child or baby. You can realize that the person in the photo suffers or did suffer, like you do. You can bring up compassion toward them by wishing for their suffering to end and for them to be happy and safe. Try to match these feelings of *metta* with any bodily sensations you have in the chest/abdomen area. With practice, metta can open up the heart and mind and allow us to feel deeply and with appreciation our connection to ourselves and others.

APPENDIX 2: MEDITATION POSTURES

Kneeling on a cushion

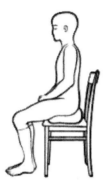

Sitting in a chair

Sitting on a cushion with legs folded in front

ABBREVIATIONS

DN – Digha Nikaya
Dhp – Dhammapada
Iti - Itivuttaka
MN – Majjhima Nikaya
Sn – Sutta Nipata
SN – Samyutta Nikaya
AN – Anguttara Nikaya
Ud - Udana

GLOSSARY

Anchor – an object used to fix the attention giving it a place to repeatedly return to and rest upon. Often the breath is used as an anchor.

Buddha – The man (Siddatha Gotoma) who became enlightened, taught the *Dhamma*, and established the community of practitioners (*Sangha*) 2500 years ago.

Brahmaviharas – the 4 Divine Abodes or 4 immeasurable qualities; positive qualities of the heart/mind that can be intentionally cultivated: lovingkindess (*metta*), compassion (*karuna*), sympathetic joy (*mudita*), and equanimity (*upekkha*).

Dana – giving or generosity; an important quality of the heart and mind to cultivate.

Dhamma – (*Dharma* in *Sanskrit*) The Buddha's teachings; truth; the law of the universe. When in the plural (*dhammas*), it can mean the 4th foundation of mindfulness.

Dukkha – Suffering; stress; unsatisfactoriness.

Hindrance – one of 5 mental factors that obstructs mindfulness and concentration (see page 56).

Kalyana mitta – Spiritual friend; one who is a companion and support on the path of meditation practice.

Kamma – (*karma* in *Sanskrit*) Intention; volitional action; The universal law of action and results: Skillful intention leads to happiness, unskillful intention leads to suffering. The results of *kamma* influence rebirth.

Khandha – the 5 aggregates (of clinging); the Buddha's classification scheme of our entire physical-mental experience; the 5 are: form, feeling tones, perceptions, formations, and conscsiousness.

Mara – The personification of the defilements; the king of death in Buddhist cosmology.

Metta – Lovingkindness; one of the *Brahmaviharas* (Divine Abodes); positive regard for and good-will toward ourselves and others.

Nibbana – (*Nirvana* in *Sanskrit*) Enlightenment; awakening; liberation; the deathless; unbinding; cessation of suffering and the round of rebirths; the extinguishment of greed, hatred, and delusion; the complete relinquishment of the defilements.

Pali – Ancient Indian language through which the teachings of the Buddha were transmitted; related to Sanskrit.

Panna – Wisdom, one of the 3 trainings of the Buddhist path.

Papanca – The proliferation of discursive thoughts and ideas.

Sangha – The original community of enlightened monks and nuns during the Buddha's time. The term is now more widely applied to the community of Buddhist practitioners both locally and globally.

Samsara – The cycle of suffering and rebirths subject to the law of *kamma*.

Samadhi – Concentration; focus; unity of mind; one of the 3 trainings of the Buddhist path and one of the noble eightfold path factors.

Sati – Mindfulness; one of the noble eightfold path factors.

Satipatthana – The 4 foundations or establishments of mindfulness.

Sankhara – Mental formations; fabrications; volitional formations; the 4th of the 5 aggregates.

Sila – Ethical conduct; morality; one of the 3 trainings of the Buddhist path.

Tipitika – The "Three Baskets" of teachings: *Vinaya*, *Sutta*, and *Abhidhamma*; the Pali Canon.

Vedana – Feeling tone(s); the 2nd foundation of mindfulness; the 2nd of the 5 aggregates.

Vinaya – the Buddha's teachings on moral discipline; the monastic rules of conduct.

ACKNOWLEDGEMENTS

I am grateful to the years of support that I have received from my many teachers. I especially wish to acknowledge Gil Fronsdal, John Travis, the Venerable Bhikkhu Bodhi, the Venerable Thanissaro Bhikkhu, Tony Bernhard, and Andrew Olenzdki. Their wisdom and counsel has sheltered me from much mishap and unskillful practice. Dennis Warren, the founder of SIM, has shown me longstanding kindness, generosity, and wisdom. Without his guidance and vision, there would be no SIM and I would not have the honor and merit of being a community mentor at SIM. My fellow mentors, Rich Howard and Diane Wilde have also been kind and patient teachers and companions in keeping the *Dhamma* at SIM skillful and beneficial. My family (my mother, father, and sisters) has been supportive of my practice and continues to teach me about love. Jenny Mueller, my beloved partner, has been an invaluable source of wisdom, joy, and counsel. Her editorial assistance on this manuscript is deeply appreciated. I am very grateful for her kindness, patience, wisdom, and generosity. I also thank our two cats, Sammie and Bubbi who continually challenge me to practice. Finally, I am grateful to all the former and present members of SIM who have been supportive of my practice and tolerant of my follies. Thank you for your efforts. I am continually inspired by your practice.

ABOUT THE AUTHOR

Jeff Hardin has been practicing Insight Meditation since 2000. He is a community mentor at the Sacramento Insight Meditation group and sits on the boards of the Sati Center for Buddhist Studies and the Folsom Prison Sangha. He is a volunteer for Buddhist Global Relief and a founding member of Insight World Aid, two non-profit organizations that aspire to transform the Buddha's teachings into social benefit. He has graduated from SIM's Practice Development and Leadership Program and is enrolled in Spirit Rock Meditation Center's Community Dharma Leadership Program. He studies the early discourses (*suttas*) of the Buddha. He is a practicing physician in Sacramento, CA.

ADDITIONAL RESOURCES

Books

The Issue at Hand by Gil Fronsdal, 2001. A collection of well-written essays about meditation practice by a Spirit Rock teacher. Available for free at: www.insightmeditationcenter.org.

In the Buddha's Words: An Anthology of Discourses from the Pali Canon, edited by Bhikkhu Bodhi, 2005, Wisdom Publications. A great introduction to the suttas and an overview of the Buddha's teachings.

An Introduction to Buddhism by Peter Harvey, 1990, Cambridge University Press. A classic textbook on the world of Buddhism.

Satipatthana: The Direct Path to Realization by Analayo, 2003, Windhorse Publications. A scholarly and comprehensive treatise on the practice of the 4 foundations of mindfulness.

The Noble Eightfold Path: The Way to End Suffering, by Bhikkhu Bodhi, 2000, BPS Pariyati Editions. An excellent, concise book on the Buddha's path. Available online for free: www.accesstoinsight.org.

Insight Meditation: The Practice of Freedom by Joseph Goldstein, 1993, Shambhala Publications. A skillful overview of insight meditation by one of the founders of the insight meditation movement in the West.

Lovingkindness: The Revolutionary Art of Happiness by Sharon Salzberg, 2004, Shambhala Publications. A classic, beautifully written book on the practice of metta by one of the pioneers of the insight meditation movement.

The Life and Teachings of the Buddha: An Introductory Sutta Study Guide by Jeff Hardin, 2010, self-published. A primer on reading the *suttas* and the main tenets of the *Dhamma*. Available in PDF format for free at www.sactoinsight.org.

Online/Correspondence Courses

Insight Meditation: An In-depth Correspondence Course. Available through Sounds True. An excellent, yearlong experiential course that includes CDs, a workbook, and correspondence with a teacher: www.soundstrue.com.

Introduction to Mindfulness, taught by Gil Fronsdal and Ines Freedman of the Insight Meditation Center. Ongoing courses in meditation with mentor support or available for audit. www.insightmeditationcenter.org.

Audio

SIM Dharma Talks. Audio files on meditation topics by SIM teachers and mentors: www.sactoinsight.org/res_med_dharmatalks.

Audio Dharma. Audio files on meditation topics by Gil Fronsdal, Andrea Fella and other insight meditation teachers: www.audiodharma.org.

Dharma Seed. Audio files on meditation topics by insight meditation teachers from Insight Meditation Society and the Spirit Rock Meditation Center: www.dharmaseed.org.

Websites

Sacramento Insight Meditation. Meditation instructions, audio files on dharma talks, and the current schedule of events: www.sactoinsight.org.

Insight Meditation Center of Redwood City. Site for essays, audio talks, and other support for meditation by Gil Fronsdal and other insight meditation teachers: www.insightmeditationcenter.org.

Insight Meditation Society, Barre Massachusetts. Meditation support and meditation retreats: www.dharma.org.

The Spirit Rock Meditation Center, Woodacre California. Meditation support and meditation retreats: www.spiritrock.org.

Access to Insight. A collection of essays on various Buddhist topics and suttas translated into English. www.accesstoinsight.org.

Buddhist Publication Society. Online versions of essays and books on Buddhist topics: www.bps.lk/index.asp

Journals

The Inquiring Mind. A journal for the insight meditation community. www.inquiringmind.com.

The Insight Journal. An excellent collection of articles related to the study and practice of the *Dhamma* published by the Barre Center for Buddhist Studies. www.dharma.org/ij.

The Sati Journal. A publication of the Sati Center for Buddhist Studies that advocates the use of *Dhamma* study to inform meditation practice. Volume 1 to be published in Winter 2011. www.sati.org.

INDEX

Made in the USA
Charleston, SC
28 January 2013